Sail The World

Sail The World

The Jubilee Sailing Trust

JUBILEE SAILING TRUST
changing lives

© The Jubilee Sailing Trust, 2016

Published by The Jubilee Sailing Trust

A CIP catalogue record for this book is available from the British Library.

ISBN 978-0-9516334-3-4

Book layout and jacket design by Clare Brayshaw

Jacket photo and endpapers by Marcin Dobrowolski

Prepared and printed by:

York Publishing Services Ltd
64 Hallfield Road
Layerthorpe
York YO31 7ZQ

Tel: 01904 431213

Website: www.yps-publishing.co.uk

Contents

BUCKINGHAM PALACE

I am delighted to be able to introduce this book on the voyages of the STS Lord Nelson.

In 2012, the Lord Nelson began its remarkable journey to take a mixed ability crew on a global circumnavigation sailing adventure which involved more than 1000 voluntary crew members and took almost 2 years to complete. The Jubilee Sailing Trust was therefore able to spread its message of inclusion and diversity to 30 countries across the World as well as teaching the invaluable skills of teamwork and leadership to its volunteers.

I would like to express my congratulations to everyone on a remarkable voyage. This book celebrates the successes as well as describing the challenges faced by the crew as Lord Nelson sailed 50,000 miles around the world highlighting the wonderful and inspiring work of the Jubilee Sailing Trust.

Acknowledgements

There are many people to thank for their help, without whose efforts this book could have not been produced. My sincere thanks:

To those who provided articles for their voyages. In particular, a huge thank you to the two Captains Barbara Campbell and Chris Phillips.

To the people who placed the thousands of photos on the voyage CDs. I have tried to give a credit to those whose photos I have used, but many of the details were not listed on the CDs. My sincere apologies for not giving the credit where due.

The big worry about producing this book was the initial cost involved. Many people know Chrissie Parsons and her husband Andy. Chrissie formed the JST 2-6 Heavers branch in London over 25 years ago, and is now their President. She is a hugely-valued Ambassador for the Trust, and both she and Andy visited many of the countries at their own expense to meet *Lord Nelson*, and help organise the port visits. Following the recent death of Andy's mother, they have very generously agreed to give part of her legacy to the Trust to sponsor the book, a cause which Andy's mother would have been more than happy to approve.

To director David Mercer and his staff from York Publishing Services for producing this book at cost. David sails with the JST as a Watch Leader, and was a crew member on Leg 7. David gave all his own time for free.

To my wife Molly, for her invaluable assistance proof-reading the articles.

To the late Keith Bacon who provided the drawings for the title page and the compass rose used for each leg. These were actually the drawings used for the JST tankards but Keith, who was a staunch supporter of the JST, died suddenly before he finished the book artwork.

To the companies below for their generous support, and my apologies for missing anyone:

Norton Rose Fulbright – For sponsoring the project, both financially and with legal assistance.

The Nautical Institute – Their world-wide network of members was asked for assistance. Many gave valuable help; most notably free pilotage was provided in Rio de Janeiro, saving thousands of dollars.

Dryad Maritime – Provided free pre-voyage security planning, and 24-hour monitoring through the pirate risk areas of the Indian Ocean, Malacca Strait, and until out of the Indonesian waters.

Spearfish – Onboard security services through the Indian Ocean.

UK Hydrographic Office – Provided pre StW planning charts, and supported the ship worldwide.

Thomas Gunn Navigation Services Ltd.

PMPT Ltd – Weather routing for major passages and 24-hour monitoring for Tropical Cyclones through the Indian Ocean.

Globecomm – For providing the Iridium Satellite communication system.

Association of British Ports Southampton – Provided free berthing and use of the QEII terminal for the send-off party.

Introduction by Alan Fisher

The Jubilee Sailing Trust (JST) is a registered charity based in Southampton UK, which owns and operates two tall ships, *STS Lord Nelson* and *SV Tenacious*. Both *Lord Nelson* and *Tenacious* were built in the UK with the capability of sailing anywhere in the world with mixed physical ability crews aboard. The history of the JST can be found on www.jst.org.uk.

In November 2011 Alex Lochrane, the previous Chief Executive of the JST, and Andy Spark, the Ship Operations Manager, were at the Sail Training International conference in Toulon. It was there that they heard of the Australian invitation for ships to attend their International Fleet Review in Sydney in 2013, to celebrate the 100th anniversary of the Royal Australian Navy's fleet first sailing into Sydney. People at the conference from all over the world came up to them and said "No one else does what the JST does – why don't you send one of your ships to visit us so our disabled people can go sailing?" Andy had always

Alan Fisher

dreamed of sailing one of the ships round the world, but would it be possible to take part? The myriad of difficulties to be overcome in such a short time frame made it an extremely daunting task, but nothing ventured, nothing gained, so they took the plunge and accepted the invitation. Thus was born the Sail the World adventure on *Lord Nelson*.

The ship left from the home port of Southampton on Trafalgar Day, 21 October 2012, returning to Southampton on 26 September 2014. It became an epic voyage of 11 legs and 19 intermediate voyages, involving more than 1,000 volunteer crew comprising both able-bodied and disabled people. Norton Rose (later Norton Rose Fulbright), a global law firm, generously became the sponsor for this Sail the World challenge.

I was fortunate enough to sail as a Bosun's Mate on three voyages and the final leg back from Halifax Nova Scotia. I recently found myself reminiscing about *Lord Nelson's* triumphant return to London

STS Lord Nelson

SV Tenacious

in 2014. We sailed under Tower Bridge to a fanfare from the trumpeters of the Band of HM Royal Marines; we were welcomed by our friends and families that we hadn't seen for six weeks; and, to cap it all, we enjoyed a fantastic party given by the project sponsors in their offices overlooking Tower Bridge. What a wonderful return to our first port of call in the UK!

This journey of adventure in the 21st century on a tall ship would soon be forgotten if it wasn't formally recorded – someone should write a book about it, but who? It would have to be a volunteer with plenty of time, someone who knows the JST and its staff, and someone who took part. Could I do it? Well, why not? Someone has to.

So here it is, not so much written by me, but compiled from the stories and photographs of those voyagers involved.

Alan Fisher

The Captains

Captain Barbara Campbell

Captain Barbara Campbell, who lives in Dunoon, Scotland, went to sea in 1975 as a Deck Cadet with P&O Steam Navigation Co and took her Foreign-Going Masters' Certificate in Glasgow in 1986.

Barbara passed a personal milestone in 2015, as it was the 40th year of her long sea-going career. Barbara was one of P&O's first female cadets. She has sailed as Captain for the last 17 years.

Following a conventional four-year cadetship, largely in cargo ships, Barbara then worked for P&O Cruises and P&O Scottish Ferries until 1995. She joined the Jubilee Sailing Trust in 1996, sailing as Mate in *Lord Nelson* for three years.

In February 1999 Barbara was very proud to gain her first command and become Master of the schooner *Malcolm Miller*, run by the Sail Training Association. The offer of command with the Jubilee Sailing Trust tempted Barbara back to the JST in 2002 and since then she has been Master of both *Lord Nelson* and *Tenacious*. Barbara's husband Chris has been heard to say "I wish she could manoeuvre our car as well as she manoeuvres the ship!".

In 2004, Barbara was inducted as a Younger Brother of Trinity House, on the same day as The Princess Royal. Barbara was awarded the Merchant Navy Medal in 2007, for Meritorious Service. She is also an examiner for the Nautical Institute's 'International Sailing Endorsement Scheme'. Barbara received the Victoria Drummond Award in 2015, (named after the first

Photo: Max Mudie

female Chief Engineer in the British Merchant Navy) for her achievements at sea.

Barbara has inspired and encouraged many young men and women to follow in her footsteps. Several of these are currently serving as officers with a variety of shipping companies. Barbara has given advice to those seeking to work at sea professionally, as well as to Merchant Navy Cadets, who frequently sail on board *Lord Nelson* and *Tenacious*. Barbara felt very privileged to be in command of *Lord Nelson* for 25,332 nautical miles of her Sail the World voyage.

Following a rough crossing of the Bass Strait, between Melbourne and Hobart, Barbara received an accolade from a lady crew member in a wheelchair: "It's empowering to see a woman do what she loves, in a typically man's profession, and do it well. Having a female Captain made the voyage even more special for me. I was impressed by her calm confidence, boldness and ability to take us all on an amazing adventure".

Captain Christopher John Phillips

Captain Chris Phillips is a career seafarer with a wide variety of experience in the Merchant and Royal Navies. His seafaring career started when he was taken dinghy sailing as a baby still in his carry-cot; sailing featured heavily during his childhood, both with his family and at school.

Early ambitions to join HM Diplomatic Service, or one of the other prestigious organisations operating overseas, took him to Exeter University to read French and Russian, and it was whilst a student that he first sailed as a trainee in the Sail Training Association's three-masted topsail schooner *STS Malcolm Miller*. This trip awakened his seafaring genes, and a further voyage as trainee saw him recommended to join the afterguard as a volunteer Watch Officer. Within a couple of years he had risen in the hierarchy to sail as relief Bosun during his last summer at university. The same summer he also spent a few weeks as an able seaman in his first square-rigged ship, the Dutch *Barque Europa*.

By this time his career plans had changed, and he had opted for a career at sea. Coming from a Royal Naval family, the RN was an obvious option, but he also explored the possibility of a Merchant Navy cadetship. As it turned out, at the time very few shipping companies were recruiting youngsters of graduate age, and although he was offered a place in a small company mainly operating in the offshore industry, he opted for the more familiar surroundings of the RN, joining Britannia Royal Naval College in September 1998. He passed a more or less happy year at the College, thoroughly enjoying his time playing in boats on the river Dart. Having already gained his RYA Yachtmaster ticket, he was soon given the custody of one of the College yachts, and was usually seen on Wednesday afternoons and at weekends taking new entry officer Cadets out sailing in Start and Tor bays, a pastime that earned him the College's newly-inaugurated Wiluna Prize for seamanship.

On passing out from Dartmouth, he suffered an unfortunate injury in a sea boat during a fishery patrol which was followed by a frustrating period of shore jobs

Photo: Gene Wan

interspersed with the odd period at sea, more time in hospital, and rehabilitation. This period of uncertainty did allow him a few "jollies", most notably a three-month trip in the Argentine sail training ship *Libertad*, at once a most interesting experience from the military, diplomatic and seafaring perspectives.

On his return from Argentina, Chris qualified as an Officer of the Watch (OOW) and found himself unexpectedly appointed to the Submarine Service. A short gap between courses enabled him to take a transatlantic round trip as a supernumerary in a refrigerated cargo ship, loading bananas in Central America. More courses followed before joining HM Submarine *Vigilant* in Faslane Naval Base. The start of his time in *Vigilant* was not happy, and it was at this stage that Chris decided that it would soon be time for him and the RN to part company. Before this could happen, however, he qualified as a submariner, went on two strategic deterrent patrols and attended the Fleet Navigators course, finishing his time on board as a watch navigator and responsible for not losing any of the ship's cryptographic material.

In parallel with his RN career, Chris had kept up his time in sail training vessels, as volunteer 3rd Officer, relief 2nd Officer and relief Bosun in the Sail Training Association's new Brigs, *Stavros S Niarchos* and *Prince William*. Encouraged by Captain Barbara Campbell, he also tested the water with the JST, sailing twice as a supernumerary Deck Officer in their barque *Lord Nelson*.

On his release from the Royal Navy in spring 2005, Chris spent some time gaining civilian qualifications before joining the JST. Apart from a brief two-week trip in an aggregate dredger, and six months at college gaining his OOW (unlimited) ticket, he has been with the JST ever since, soon rising to Chief Officer rank, and spending his time in both JST ships around Northern Europe, the Mediterranean and the Canaries. A short trip as Master of *Lord Nelson* in July 2011 led to his permanent promotion to Master in January 2012. He spent much of 2012-14 on the Sail the World deployment, and has recently returned from his first trip as Master of *Tenacious* in the South Pacific.

Chris also spends much of his leisure time at sea in his traditionally-rigged ketch *Meander*, and having crossed the Atlantic (west-east) two-handed in her in 2009, was awarded the Royal Naval Sailing Association's Tim Sex Trophy for an outstanding act of seamanship in an offshore yacht. In 2015 he was invested as a Yeoman of Trinity House.

Chris is single, lives in Gosport (when not on board *Meander*), enjoys a good read, walking in the hills, playing the bodhran and singing shanties.

JUBILEE SAILING TRUST
changing lives

Pre-Voyage Maintenance and Departure from Southampton

by Captain Barbara Campbell

For an onlooker to have seen *Lord Nelson* on 18 October, the day I joined, and just one day before the Voyage Crew (VC) joined, they could be forgiven for thinking that the ship was in the middle of a major refit, rather than in a state of readiness for the greatest undertaking of her life!

Equipment, tools and gear were piled in every available space following a four-week maintenance and refit programme. "Stuff" was dumped on deck, in lifts, in cabins and in the Chartroom. The tables of the lower mess were stacked metres high with kit. More worryingly, the two new generators, which had just been fitted, had not been run-up or tested. It seemed impossible that we would get the bunks clear for the Voyage Crew.

Photo: Captain Barbara Campbell

As always, the Permanent Crew and the volunteers went the extra mile, working all hours and by the following morning, the ship looked in a half-decent state. I say "looked", as behind the scenes, the new generators had not been fully tested; three roller furling stays had yet to be rigged and the sails bent on; the ship was in further disarray with air-conditioning units being retro-fitted everywhere.

David (Taff) James – Maintainer storing 'stuff'.

I felt distinctly apprehensive. It was all very well being caught up in the euphoria and excitement of all around, but I was in charge of taking the ship and her crew to sea. My comments to the CEO that the ship was not ready did not go down well. In truth, the desire to keep the departure date as 21 October meant that we were not as prepared as we should have been. However, for me, the weather forecasts tipped the balance of whether or not to sail. There was a great weather-window for sailing across the Bay of Biscay and too good an opportunity to miss. As a date, the 21 October could not be bettered. Our departure was set for 1150, as this was the very time, on that day in 1805, that the flag-hoist "Make all sail possible with safety to the masts" was sent from *HMS Victory* to the entire British Fleet, just prior to the Battle of Trafalgar.

Photo: Alan Fisher

When the VC joined on the 19th, most of the accommodation spaces had been cleared and scrubbed, and new duvets and bed linen brightened the place up. The main deck was filthy, as we had only managed a cursory sweep. Not only was it VC joining day, but it was also media day for the global law firm Norton Rose (later to become Norton Rose Fulbright), hence the name, "Norton Rose Sail the World Challenge". At the last moment we had "title sponsors". I was presented with a flag and a chart by one of our vice-patrons, the broadcaster Peter Snow.

The following morning several of us had an 0530 start. We wanted to take advantage of the state of the tide to bring back aboard the heavy ropes and sails from the shore-side container, via the mid-ships gangway gate.

Jon West, the Mate, did a great job of VC training whilst so much was going on all around. The engineers ran up the new generators, whilst on deck last-minute stores were brought on board, and the Outer Jib and Mizzen

Staysails were bent on. The VC had the afternoon off to buy any last-minute bits and pieces, and we shifted ship at 1630 to the QE2 terminal for our big farewell party that evening.

Sunday 21st October, Sailing Day. Whilst Marcin Dobrowolski, 2nd Mate, ran though Seamanship and Yard bracing with the Voyage Crew, the rest of us tidied up the decks, making all secure for sea. Due to complications with the roller furling gear, the mizzen staysail was sent down and back up again. The engineers continued working on the generators and readying the main engines.

I gathered all the VC below decks as I felt I had not had much chance to talk with them. I wanted to say a few words about severing the physical ties with the land, and that during the course of the voyage, we would need to look after each other and be mindful of our, at times, great distance from shore.

Photo: Alan Fisher

A large crowd of well-wishers, office staff, friends and family were on the quayside to see us off, plus a few people from our title sponsors. I was delighted that we were presented with a Paralympian torch from the 2012 London Olympics, just before we landed the gangway. For the crossing of the Bay of Biscay I was to share my bunk with this precious torch, as I felt it the safest place in the ship! After the gangway was landed, Juliet Howland sang the song "Good Luck", followed by the Missions to Seamen padré who gave a blessing. The blessing was slightly longer than expected, however, making us a couple of minutes late on our 1150 departure. We motored up Southampton Water, turned around, picked up the RIB and sailed back past the QE2 berth and our well-wishers, with the Topsails and T'Gallants set. The tug *Sarah* was in attendance using her fire-fighting water jets to dramatic effect. The whistles blew and final farewells called.

Photo: Alan Fisher

We made good progress out of Southampton Water, set the Fore Course and turned the engines off in the Needles Channel, making a good 5 knots. We sailed overnight with the wind on the starboard quarter. It had been an emotional send-off but it felt good to be at sea, and great to be under sail again.

In the north of the Bay of Biscay, a mere two days later, in surprisingly benign conditions and light NE winds, it felt a different world from the noise and chaos of Southampton.

Photo: Alan Fisher

Leg 1

Southampton to Rio de Janeiro by Captain Barbara Campbell

On 23rd October, 50 miles to the west of Ushant, in light winds and clear of all traffic, we stopped the ship head-to-wind in order to send up the Main Topmast Staysail. At 1600 we set sails and rang 'Finished with Engines' at 2100. It was definitely a good move to sail as the wind steadily picked up overnight to an E'ly force 5 by 0700. For the remainder of the day we sailed at 7 knots and everyone appreciated both the weather and great sailing in the Bay of Biscay.

Five days of continuous good sailing ensued and we rounded Cape Finisterre at 1100 on 26th. The wind slowly backed NNE'ly and we adjusted our course to minimise rolling. On the 27th the wind touched force 6, giving us an average speed of 7 knots with bursts of up to 9 knots. Whoopee! We even had our first glimpse of the sun. This day also had the distinction of being the last day our foul weather gear was needed.

On the 28th, accompanied by Bosun's Mate (BM) Kirsten on violin, we held a Sunday service on deck. Late afternoon the wind fell light as forecast, and at 1600 we clewed up sail and motored on. By the following day, although the sea was flat calm, the long ocean swell set us rolling once more. I gave the first of my Celestial Navigation talks and by the time the watch had worked out noon, my brain was just about frazzled – our Voyage Crew (VC) not being chosen for their ability to subtract one number from another!

Late afternoon on the 29th the power supply to the main radar failed. This was a major problem, but thanks to our engineers, we located the defective parts and after checking with Sperry using our satellite phone, ordered spares that same day. Our secondary radar was very much yacht-style, with the picture on a computer screen. It was excellent at what it was meant to do, but with an inadequate range and bearing facility, a fuzzy picture and poor definition, it was in no way a replacement for our 'high spec' main radar.

We began to feel the ship rise and fall with the swell from the SW which heralded strong SW winds. The following day I had wanted to motor-sail with the fore-and-aft sails set, to minimise the motion, i.e. sail with the wind 30 to 40 degrees off the bow. As the top swivel of the recently refurbished Outer Jib furling gear failed to function, I decided to set the Inner Jib. This is a hanked-on sail but the running rigging was not in place. Together with Lesley the Bosun and the BMs, I went forward to help with this. At 0900, when we started setting the sail, the wind was NE force 2, with the bowsprit rising and falling gently in the swell. Before we got the sail properly set, the wind had increased to force 5, and despite our slowing down, the seas became really lumpy. Whilst I had a team behind me on the halyard, Lesley and the BMs were getting a real dunking on the bow. A loss of control of the Inner Jib sheet meant we had to haul the sail back to deck straight away. Not quite beaten, we set the Main Staysail which helped improve the motion. The seas became wild and we felt many sharp slaps against the ship's side, caused by waves of several tonnes of water being thrown against the ship. By 1500 the wind

was astern, even though the swell was from ahead. We squared the fore yards and set the Fore Topsail. Instantly this helped lift the bow and improve speed and motion. The sky cleared and Jupiter, together with the stars of the summer triangle, shone clear above.

The following morning we clewed up the Fore Topsail and continued motoring to Las Palmas. The SSW winds were from an unusual direction, with no sign of the NE trade wind. During this time the engineers worked ceaselessly on the generators and air conditioning (AC), together with all the on-going maintenance. In addition to our two permanent engineers, we carried three extra engineering hands to help with all the work required.

Gran Canaria was in view by dawn on 2nd November, and, with time in hand, we executed a man-overboard drill whilst awaiting the pilot. A good night was had ashore by all, except the poor Captain who was duty officer! My original plan had been to allow four days in Las Palmas, giving time for the radar to be fixed, the AC parts to arrive, the annual Lloyds Surveys, and for topping up food stores. We were not impressed to find that the AC components, though not a show-stopper, were not due into Las Palmas until the 6th, the day I was planning on sailing! At least our new Main Royal sail was waiting for us. We fixed the swivel problem with the Outer Jib and adjusted the other roller-furling stays. The new Main Royal sail was bent on aloft and it felt good to have a complete set of sails once again. Our four days in Las Palmas slowly stretched to six. In one way it was frustrating, but the main thing was that we were getting important work done. The new radar parts were installed, but the unit steadfastly refused to work and more parts were ordered.

On 8th November, the radar spares and the last of our AC pipework finally arrived. Customs in Madrid held up a box of medical stores and a box of charts and we ended up sailing without them. Jim Phillips, 2nd Mate on leave, and our electronics whizz, lives in Gran Canaria. He was a star and came down and fitted the radar part that very day. None of us felt that it had really cured the problem. However the radar was working as required. Gaskets on the square sails were released and we singled-up ready to leave the berth. After six days of being tethered to the quay I was determined to sail off the berth without engine assistance. We let go all but one stern-line and set the Fore Topsail. The stern-line was let go as the Fore Course was being set, so that we would have enough sail area forward in order to be able to steer. It worked a treat, and we continued setting sail as we left the harbour. By the time we reached the outer breakwater we had all the square sails set on the foremast and the Topsail and T'Gallant set on the mainmast. Kirsten, BM, and the VC linesmen ashore said we looked magnificent as we sailed off. It was a shame there was no one with video equipment there to record it. The wind was NNE force 4 as we set our southerly course. Once more it was great to be at sea.

For the first time I felt that we could get into a good daily routine, and I continued the Celestial Navigation classes with the VC. Just two days out of Las Palmas

Hoisting spare sails on board prior to departure, Southampton.

the Sperry radar for which we had long awaited a part, 'crashed' and became inoperable. That was the last time that radar worked before Rio! The noon watch took sun sights to work out noon, with some of the VC getting really good results. The GPS was only out by 0.1 mile some days! The days got steadily warmer as we headed south.

On Remembrance Sunday we held a lovely service on the foredeck, largely organised by Steve Ogden, Medical Purser, and aided by the two marines, injured servicemen who were on board through the charity 'Help for Heroes'. One of the marines read the Royal Marine prayer, followed by two minutes' silence. 'Reveillé' was played, a home-made wreath thrown overboard, and Kirsten played the violin for hymns, including "Onward Christian Soldiers". That afternoon we passed the 2,000 mile mark, averaging 7 knots in great down-wind sailing with the wind ENE force 6.

Remembrance Sunday – Wreath before being cast into the sea.

The temperature was climbing below decks, with temperatures reaching 30 degrees in the foc's'le accommodation and Permanent Crew (PC) cabins, as the AC was not yet operational in these areas. With the sea temperature at 28 degrees it was difficult to keep cool. The aft deckhouse was being prepped for painting – there is a lot of it to scrape and sand! All volunteers were welcomed by Bosun Lesley and her team, armed with scrapers, sand paper and good music. Jenny, Chief

Engineer, had a mammoth task on her hands as she progressed with extensive engineering works. She felt she was 'mid-marathon', with Chipps, 2nd Engineer, also kept hard at work.

With the wind blowing a steady force 4 to 6 from the North East, we were enjoying some great sailing and looked splendid under virtually full sail. It was a shame that only our crew and the occasional passing fishing boat were witness to the sight. Around us the sea sparkled and the deep ocean swell gave the ship a continuous easy roll. At night the spangly green and white phosphorescence pulsated down the ship's side. It was a long passage but no-one was bored. We trimmed the yards and tried to get the best speed out of the ship. Cookie Dave and Cook's Assistant Margaret looked forward to an end of exploding fridges, meringue-plastered ovens and chilli on the hob! We trailed fishing lines in the hope of a fresh catch, and I promised Cookie that I would make sushi with the first fish. The Milky Way was as clear as it could be. We played a game of 'Murder', when I sneakily persuaded Jon, the Mate, to do rounds a day early and went on to 'murder' him on the stern platform with a scrubbing brush. Ha! Much plotting and 'killing' ensued with the whole crew participating.

We required an average speed of almost 6 knots so we had to motor when the wind was light; e.g. if we were sailing at 3 knots, we would keep the sails set and motor on one engine, to make about 7 knots. On 18th November, at latitude 8 degrees north, we completely lost the wind and ended up handing all sail. Sporadic showers were visible around us. As dinner was being cleared up we encountered our first major tropical downpour. Mate Jon made the tannoy announcement "Due to unforeseen circumstances there are showers on deck; feel free to use them for as long as you wish". Most of the VC who were not already on deck dashed up, several taking Jon at his word, and out came the shampoo and conditioner. One of the VC had her long hair washed in the scuppers by Jenny the Chief Engineer. The downpour lasted ten minutes leaving behind a lumpy sea under leaden skies, and a clean refreshed crew!

Photo: Captain Barbara Campbell

Both Lesley and Jon were badly affected by the temperature. When the heat in the PC cabins became excessive, Lesley slept on the office floor! Her favourite method of cooling down was to wring out a wet towel and lay it over herself, whilst lying naked on her bunk under the fan. Lesley and Jon dreamed of ice and cold, and both looked 'wrung out' most of the time. BM Neil, MP Steve, Jon the Mate and various crew were helping with the massive job of lagging all the AC pipework. Even I spent an afternoon stuffed in an awkward corner of the galley store, cutting and fitting the lagging. Getting the AC going was our aim. The biggest problem was that with insufficient lagging, we had lots of condensation on the pipes and on the inside of the hull. The engineers had tested all sections of the AC system to prove they worked, but could not run them for any length of time until the lagging task was completed.

As we approached the equator, big preparations were underway for the "Crossing the Line" ceremony. We crossed into Southern Realms at 1141 on 22nd November with the chartroom packed: all were eager to see the GPS showing the magical latitude of 00° 00.0′. We 'Shellbacks', those who had crossed the line before, had great fun organising the ceremony. The costumes were made and crimes identified for all the 'Pollywogs' – those who had not crossed the equator by sea before. As King Neptune, I worked long into the

Catch of the day. The Captain or the fish?

night polishing my trident, trimming my beard and preparing for the ascent of my 'court' from our caves on the Ocean floor. Just as well I had my snorkel fins on, as it is a long ascent from a depth of 4,000 metres!

My lovely wife, Queen Neptunia, aka Jon, came with me. She wanted to show off her new fish-net stockings and coral-pink nail varnish. I had been summoned by the Pirate King, Cookie Dave, who had taken over the ship *Lord Nelson*. He had locked all the PC in the hot sweaty galley store. From the darkest depths came other members of my court: the Surgeon, aka Steve, Medical Purser; the Barber, Taffy; Chief of Police was Jenny the Chief Engineer, aided by three VC who had previously crossed the line and were Constables. When Pirate Dave took the ship, he kidnapped the well-endowed Captain's daughter, 2nd Mate, Marcin.

Once the 'court' was assembled around the pool, the pollywogs were rounded up by the police and brought to Neptune's court. They had their crimes read out, were found guilty and accepted their punishment. The cries of 'guilty, guilty' were shouted out by the rest of the VC. One by one, the 'pollywogs' got on their knees

in the children's paddling pool to show due respect to Neptune and Neptunia. Then they had to 'kiss the fish'. That fish, purchased in Las Palmas market, turned out to be the best 1.81 euros I have ever spent! Steve, the Surgeon, administered 'medicine', usually a spoonful of baked beans and a vile drink syringed into the mouth. Taffy, the Barber, used copious amounts of shaving foam and coloured gunk before 'shaving' the 'pollywogs'. The Captain's daughter swanned around showing off her ample bosom. I leave you to imagine the colour of the water in the pool at the end!

Neptune and his Queen, before 'she' got badly sunburnt.

It was great that we could have so much spontaneous fun, including every single member of the crew, without alcohol being involved. One of the funniest things was that my beloved Neptunia, scrumptious though she was, foolishly forgot to apply sunscreen, and got bra-strap marks sunburned on to his shoulders – they did not go away until after he had spent New Year in Rio! The sunburn extended to his legs and he had diamond-shaped sunburn where his fish-net stockings had been! The crew declared that the ceremony had far surpassed their expectations. Although it was only the first of our 'crossing-the-line' ceremonies, those of us who took part thought that perhaps it was the best, because of the spontaneity of it all.

Early morning on 24th November we could clearly see the dramatic outline of Fernando de Noronha. The island is of volcanic origin, much of it a marine reserve.

We anchored off the tiny port, and went ashore to meet Immigration officials, who issued us with clearance papers for Brazil. The crew explored ashore; Fernando de Noronha proved to be an amazing and stunning island. Brazil aims to keep the Marine Reserve pristine, limiting numbers both on the island and also in some places in the reserve. On one special beach, numbers are restricted to twenty swimming at one time. Swimmers are not allowed to wear sunscreen while in the water, to avoid contamination of the delicate ecosystem. Several walked to the rocky NW side of the island and enjoyed the brilliant snorkelling. They all appreciated the rare opportunity to be able to visit such an isolated and unspoilt island.

Lord Nelson at anchor off Fernando de Noronha.

After two nights at anchor, we readied for sailing off the anchor without the use of engines. The manoeuvre went very well and as the anchor came aweigh, the Fore Topsail was set aback, turning the bow in the desired direction. As the ship bore away from the wind, the fore yards were braced as more sail was set on the fore and main masts. Everyone enjoyed the fact that the engines were not used at all and we were soon making 6 knots. We sailed 'Full and By' until the afternoon of 28th November when we arrived off the Brazilian port of Recife. A surprise welcoming committee of twenty from a disability group, together with local government, two TV film crews and several newspaper journalists were waiting for us. We passed cake and drinks to them across the bulwarks, whilst we tied up and rigged the gangway. Once we were secure, we had interviews and ended up with the locals coming on board, including a number in wheelchairs. The PC and several VC really helped with this, particularly as they wanted to head 'up the road'. That evening, most of the crew ended up drinking beer or caipirinhas (a local brew made from sugarcane spirit, lime and brown sugar) in the 'Sushi Bar'. This hostelry, recommended by the local police, was in a pedestrian precinct with live music and close to a police caravan. The next day was free for exploring, with the PC having a half-day following sail repairs and necessary deck or engineering work.

Happy Birthday to You!

From Recife we enjoyed good sailing in light E'ly winds down to the low-lying archipelago of Abrolhos, 30 miles off the coast of Brazil. Even the Upper Spanker got an airing on the way. The day before our arrival, I finally received authorisation for anchoring. Abrolhos means 'open your eyes' and refers to the fact that the area is a reef with just a few channels through it. It is also a reef that has claimed many ships and is now a Marine Reserve. Anchoring and landing are normally prohibited in the archipelago so we thought it brilliant that we had the Brazilian Navy's permission to do so. We anchored on the morning of 5th December, south of Santa Barbara. The only other vessel we saw was one that worked for the marine park, running dive trips. It was a delightful experience to be able to anchor in a completely unspoilt and natural place with no one else around.

As the tide, though rising, was still too low to run the crew ashore, we offered everyone the chance to swim from the ship. This was hugely successful and the water 'delicious'. We spent a happy hour swimming with nearly everyone jumping in. Cookie Dave impressed us with a dive, fully clothed (thankfully), and Beryl swam in the sea for the first time in over forty years. Frigate and Tropic birds flew overhead. The local marine staff took twelve VC snorkelling. At 1500 the tide was high enough to run the crew ashore and they were guided up to the lighthouse. In the evening we had a BBQ to which the shore staff were invited. The lighthouse keeper had to remain behind, however, but the other five enjoyed the BBQ, although they were understandably puzzled by the antics of the ensuing SODS Opera (Ship's Operatic and Drama Society), which was good fun.

The following morning we weighed anchor before breakfast, and by late afternoon were making 6 to 7 knots under sail, even after handing the Royals. The 6th December was a 'red-letter' day for many of the VC, as the AC in the foc's'le accommodation was finally on. The condensation drains from the AC were piped to a container which was emptied by the Watch every four hours. A small price to pay for AC!

On 7th December, there was a real sense of power in the sails as we chased southwards with speeds of up to 7 knots. We braced the yards at 0130 on the 8th with the Southern Cross and the Magellenic Clouds (a duo of irregular dwarf galaxies visible from the southern hemisphere) clear on our port side. The following day we closed the Brazilian coast, there was no holding *Lord Nelson* back. The wind, a NE force 6 to 7, thankfully subsided by mid-morning and, with time in hand, we sailed slowly towards Cabo Frio, handing sail in the evening.

At 0100 9th December we entered thick fog, which made big inroads into my sleep! By 0900 the fog was starting to lift but did not fully clear until we were approaching the Rio pilot station. The pilot boarded at 1200 and we could clearly see Sugarloaf and the statue of Christ. We were to berth at the submarine dock and the pilot surprised me by saying he had never been there before. We came alongside nicely and on the quayside were a few Naval officers in white uniform, plus Robbie Peacock from the JST office, and Esteves, our friendly local agent.

Our berth was at Mocangue Island, some distance from Rio. It was quickly termed 'Prison Island' by the permanent crew. Actually it was not that bad, especially from the Captain's point of view, as it was very secure and clean. There were a number of restrictions, the worst being the 1930 curfew! It took until late evening to organise transport for the crew for the following day. We found out that if the crew were in a taxi or a coach, and we informed the base in advance, then they could come back after the curfew. This we fully exploited.

Dress code was problematic as men were not allowed through the gate wearing shorts or sleeveless vests. One male VC had to come back in wearing a friend's cardigan! Every time I was called in to the Base Commander's office, (sometimes for a 'telling off' due to a perceived misdemeanour by one of our crew), I felt distinctly scruffy, despite wearing a recently-ironed white shirt and epaulettes.

We organised a minibus for the crew but it was much cheaper and often quicker to catch the bus to nearby Niteroi, followed by a 35-minute ferry to Rio. The ferry passengers did not queue exactly, but 'barged' their way along, making boarding difficult for anyone who was unsteady on their feet.

The favoured sights were the statue of Christ the Redeemer keeping a watchful eye over the people of the city, and Sugarloaf Mountain, along with the beaches of Copacabana and Ipanema. We had a great treat when we were invited to a local samba rehearsal. It was noisy to a deafening degree, but the whole place pulsed with excitement and it was difficult to remain still. About thirty of us went and it was a memorable occasion.

Everyone on board this leg of StW had a brilliant experience. This sounds like a sweeping statement, but is largely true nonetheless. We learned that long voyages can be more challenging in many ways. Much effort was put into this voyage which the VC appreciated. We enjoyed some great sailing, although we had to use engines in addition to the square sails at times in order to keep to the schedule. The bureaucracy in Rio was something to be experienced, and it was a shame that our berth was so far from the city. Hopefully our efforts in providing transport for the crew counteracted the berth difficulties.

Cook, Dave Stanley.

Photo: Sam Strong

Dates		Distances in Nautical Miles				Maximum Wind Force
Start	End	Total	Under Sail	Motor-Sailing	Motoring	
19.10.12	12.12.12	5288	2850	1198	1240	9

Voyage 11 – Rio de Janeiro to Rio de Janeiro by Captain Barbara Campbell

After various delays waiting for a pilot, we finally left the berth at 1130 on 20th December. Due to the swell, the pilot got off before we left Rio harbour. The forecast easterly wind picked up in the afternoon. We were soon making 7 knots under all square sails and having a great sail, although not everyone was enjoying it due to the swell. At 2230 we abruptly lost the wind; one minute we were making 6 knots; the next 2 knots and then nothing. We handed sail and at 2300, started motoring. At least it was a beautiful starry night.

The following morning after Happy Hour, we set sails, but had to keep one engine running to make a decent speed. We picked up a pilot for Ilhabela on the island of Sao Sebastian. It was a very simple anchoring manoeuvre and the pilot informed me that I did not need a pilot for the departure. This beautiful mountainous island was a deep green colour and very popular with folk from Sao Paulo, only a two-hour drive away. We anchored close to the Ilhabela yacht club.

Scrub, scrub, scrub!

Photo: Edison Luis Passafaro

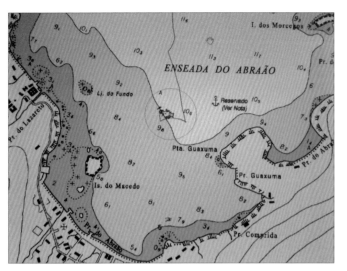

Our Christmas Day anchorage.

Photo: Edison Luis Passafaro

We had an energetic husband and wife film crew onboard, Yuri and Vera from Aventura Film. They had endless contacts and managed to organise a minibus for the crew to go the six miles to the only wheelchair accessible beach in Brazil. Yuri, a Divemaster, also organised a diving trip for six of the VC, including two wheelchair users. Yuri and Vera brought a succession of interested people like the Secretary for Tourism and newspaper reporters to the ship. The Yacht Club extended every possible courtesy, even putting their launches at our disposal and running the crew ashore and back for no payment. The crew also used the excellent Yacht Club facilities such as the pool, showers, sun loungers and, of course, the bar and restaurant. Most crew stayed ashore into the evening. A tremendous thunderstorm descended on us about 2130 and delayed the return of the VC to the ship until 2330. The downpour eased off but did not stop and we were all soaked to the skin in nice warm rain!

We weighed anchor before breakfast on 23rd and followed the scenic coast to Ilha Grande where we let go anchor in the lovely quiet bay of Sitio Forte. There are no vehicles on Ilha Grande, a stunning, mountainous, wooded island with houses dotted about. At 0830 the following morning, eight crew went diving whilst those of us on board enjoyed a swim from the ship. After lunch we weighed anchor and motored round

to the small village of Abraao, the main village on Ilha Grande. In the evening we gathered on the foredeck and sang carols, accompanied by a Watch Leader playing the flute. Mince pies were washed down with mulled wine. Strictly speaking we should have had a pilot for all our anchoring manoeuvres around Ilha Grande. My experience with pilot delays, coupled with the fact that this was Christmas, meant that, although I called the pilots on the VHF, I did not email them too, as I should have done. Our VHF calls went unanswered, as I knew they would, and I proceeded in and out without a pilot, getting my wrist gently slapped when we got back into Rio.

Calm waters off Rio.

Photo: Daphne Evans

Bucks fizz, scrambled eggs and smoked salmon ushered in Christmas day, We then ran the crew ashore to the village of Abraao. This was another very popular stop – an idyllic place for Christmas. A dozen of us set off on a two-hour hike to one of Brazil's top ten beaches. It was a tougher climb than we had expected. Some crew took the easier option of a small ferry boat round to the same brilliant beach, which consisted of sand and gentle surf, backed by trees and not a building in sight. After playing in the surf we all caught the ferry back! Other crew went to a nearby lazaretto and a waterfall, or wandered amongst the shops and bars in Abraao. At the end of the afternoon, the DOTI boat developed a problem and was towed back to the ship by a helpful local. Cookie Derek and his assistant Margaret pulled out all the stops for Christmas dinner. The PC helped serve a feast which consisted of gazpacho, turkey and all that goes with it, followed by Christmas pudding. We then had a mega washing up session. Of course our Brazilian crew had to play their part and made us Caipirinhas.

We left the serene bay of Abraao behind us, weighing anchor before breakfast on 26th and motoring towards Rio. Late afternoon we anchored just inside Punta Itaipu; it turned out to be a delightful protected anchorage and a great spot for watching the sun set against the hills of Rio. In the evening we had a BBQ, with loud thumping music which thankfully ended at 2200!

I was pleased that it was Pilot Renato who boarded for our trip back into Rio; he had helped organise free pilotage for us with the pilot company 'New Pilots'. The amount of sailing this voyage was relatively low, but the three anchorages were delightful. Amongst the small crew were seven Brazilians, including the film crew.

Tom Smith and his watch.

Photo: Daphne Evans

Two of the Brazilians commented that they felt they were being 'ordered' around and said that in Brazil you do not directly ask people to do things but instead say 'Would you like to do this?' and 'Could you possibly do that?' If we did things their way we would never have left Rio!

Rio de Janeiro to Rio de Janeiro by Janet Townend Watch Leader

Rio de Janeiro was the first official stop on the *Lord Nelson* Sail the World Challenge circumnavigation.

It all started when the JST were invited to take part in the Royal Australian Navy Anniversary in October 2013, and be part of the Tall Ships gathering and Fleet Review in Sydney.

Leg 1 was the voyage to get to Rio and Voyage 11 was the in-country voyage. We were a small crew, with a maximum of six in each watch, which meant finding enough people for anchor watches was tricky. However, the warm sunny days made up for it.

The permanent crew had been sight-seeing/shopping before we arrived and had met a member of the Rio Yacht Club. He was very interested in the conversation about *Lord Nelson* and the JST, and used his contacts

to arrange a visit for us to the Ilhabela Yacht Club (one of a few on Ilhabela).

Relaxing Ilhabela Yacht Club, *Lord Nelson* in background.

Photo: Alison Davies

When we set off from Rio we had to motor south; lack of wind was a problem throughout the voyage. Captain Barbara made use of the Brazilian couple on board to phone ahead, in Portuguese, to arrange details of where to anchor and what facilities were available to us. We were warned that we would have to anchor and be ferried ashore in the dotty boat. This would take time, and so the curfew would be at 7.30pm so that we could recover the boat before dark. However, by the time we got there, we had been offered the use of the launches with crew ALL DAY so we could stay ashore until 10pm. In fact the heavens opened just before 10pm, so we and the launch crew stayed under cover until it stopped. Everyone was late back! We were allowed to use the outdoor swimming pool which had a view of the ship, a restaurant and hot showers. Water in the Rio area was a problem as not all supplies were good enough. I assume it was something to do with shortage of water on the ship, because we were asked to make the most of the showers ashore. We enjoyed our time ashore, with walks along the coast and eating in open-air cafes.

Christmas day is always special on board with decorations and a special menu. Also the PC serve the VC. This was preceded by singing Christmas Carols, led by the Captain and accompanied by two flutes. One belonged to the ship and was played by a lady who had not played for many years.

Setting up for Christmas Day Dinner in 38°C.

Photo: Daphne Evans

Christmas Day in Rio.

Photo: Captain Barbara Campbell

As this was 2012 and was after the Olympics in London, we had the privilege of taking an Olympic torch with us on the voyage. It was held by everybody on board, and the photo I have is of a very happy partially-sighted Brazilian young man holding the torch. He had been part of the Brazilian Paralympic team (I think playing blind football). In fact he was the happiest person on board, and when he climbed aloft he had a camera on a head band so that he would be able to view his escapade when he got home.

On the way back to Rio we anchored in two different places off Ilha Grande. At one place we went ashore by dotty boat and, through connections with the Mayor, we were met by the tourist bus driven by the Head of Tourism of the local area. We were given a tour of the island and taken to some of the sights, including a very old prison dug out of the hillside. We were dropped off at a bathing spot where a river joins the sea. We all had a swim or a paddle, including Steve who normally uses a wheel chair, but managed with help to make the most of the lovely warm water. Edison from Sao Paulo, our other wheelchair user, was asked to test out the latest addition to the beach facilities, a beach buggy for wheelchair users. The Tourism Team were very pleased to be able to show it off, especially as Edison's job was making access possible for wheelchair users in hotels and public buildings.

The other event of note was the day some of the VC went scuba-diving. The Brazilian couple in my watch had some discount vouchers for a diving experience. After some negotiations six of the voyage crew and Marco, Chief Engineer and an experienced diver, went off. Again the two wheelchair users showed the way. Jon, the Mate, arranged the pulley to hoist them onto the small boat, whose roof was well below the main deck. The rest of the crew made the most of the 16°C water temperature to swim from the ship. A fun watersports day was had by all.

JST has taken me to places I never expected to visit including Antigua, The Azores, Denia (near Barcelona), Gibraltar and Malta. However, this voyage around Rio is the nearest I will get to a cruise!

Scottish shortbread for Christmas near Rio.

Photo: Edison Luis Passafaro

Dates		Distances in Nautical Miles				Maximum Wind Force
Start	End	Total	Under Sail	Motor-Sailing	Motoring	
18.12.12	27.12.12	316	57	30	229	6

Leg 2

Rio de Janeiro to Cape Town by Captain Chris Phillips

Leg 2 is the one which, of all those I captained, is the one I least wish to remember! It was marked for me by the fuel fiasco at the beginning of the voyage, which ended ten days after the ship was supposed to have departed. It started on the 29th December, which was VC joining day. The bunker barge came alongside in the morning, and presented us with a 10" hose for our 4" filling pipes. The engineers then spent the morning manufacturing an adaptor from whatever bits they could lay their hands on. This was fitted and

connected, only to find the barge master then refused to supply, due to safety concerns and time constraints, both on his part.

This started two weeks of enquiries, negotiations and delays before we actually got the fuel we needed. During this time we were able to go to anchor off Copacabana to witness a most spectacular firework display to see in the New Year 2013, and had another couple of days out for a short sail and anchorage and

New Year Fireworks, Rio.

Approaching Tristan da Cunha.

swim off Itaipu beach, just outside the filth of Rio harbour itself. For much of the rest of the time we were alongside at the Ilha de Mocangue Naval Base, far from any sort of entertainment for the crew! Eventually we had outstayed our welcome and were asked to leave the Naval Base, anchoring off Botafogo for the last couple of days whilst bunkering arrangements were finalised.

We finally left Rio on 11 January, with an average speed required of 6.5 knots to reach Cape Town on time. Needless to say, much of the voyage had to be done under engines, or with at least one or both engines running whilst under sail to maintain our speed.

There was, of course, a second excitement to the voyage, that of having to evacuate one of our wounded veterans on board, Kyle Baker, who had unfortunately developed complications with his wounds which would quickly have exhausted our supply of antibiotics. I had little option but to evacuate him, but the question, in mid-South Atlantic, was where and how? After consulting the authorities in Cape Town, it was agreed

that we would alter course towards Tristan da Cunha, two days to the south. This we did, and Kyle was safely transferred ashore from 20 miles out by their big rescue RIB. We anchored off the island a couple of hours later and stayed long enough to get our passports stamped and write postcards from this remote British outpost, before weighing and continuing at best speed towards Cape Town.

The rest of the voyage was mostly under sails and motors together, and we sighted Table Mountain in the early afternoon of the 2nd February. The last day we spent under sail in a cracking breeze, and we anchored in Table Bay in the evening, going in alongside the following morning, just in time for the VC to disembark.

Dates		Distances in Nautical Miles				Maximum Wind Force
Start	End	Total	Under Sail	Motor-Sailing	Motoring	
29.12.12	03.02.13	3537	448	2733	356	7

Rio de Janeiro to Cape Town by Lou Lyddon

The difficulties started on the 29th December 2012 when a refuelling barge tied up alongside the *Lord Nelson* to fill our nearly empty tanks. Problem one was the incompatibility of the couplings; theirs was ten inch, ours was four inch. Even the Kama Sutra couldn't solve that, so Marco's mob set to work and made an adaptor. By then it was 1130. Apparently the barge crew looked at it, muttered something about elfin safety and we got annuver job to go to and beetled off. This left us out on a limb; it was the weekend and New Year was a couple of days away. Most people seemed to be on holiday in the UK and Brazil so on the 31st we motored away from Ilha de Mocanguey and anchored about half a mile off Copacabana beach for the New Year fireworks. Those on the beach for the day may have seen the fireworks at midnight, but judging by the megawatts of music that was blasting away all day, I doubt if they ever heard them! All I can say is, 2013 started with a BANG, particularly when you were a couple of hundred yards away from a barge full of fireworks!

Crew member, Dr Liz Turner and Marco Michelagnoli.

On the 1st January 2013 we up-anchored and went back to our cosy little berth in the Brazilian Navy submarine base to start the quest for oil. Life then went through a series of ups and downs. We're getting fuel, no, we ain't, and so it went on. Apparently the British Embassy didn't want to know, so Captain Chris spent the next nine days quietly biting pieces out of his cabin door and giving us optimistic evening updates on the situation. But, as they say, all bad things come to an end and on the 9th we were told fuel was in sight and we would get it on the 11th. Unfortunately, due to the delay, the planned visit to the fabled island of Tristan da Cunha was off as we had to be in Cape Town on the 3rd February, and even that was not guaranteed. One of the two Afghan veterans on board said he couldn't stay if there was a delay, so he went back to UK.

Swimming off Itaipo beach.

On the 9th we left the berth, (my fourth departure from there) and anchored off a marina near Sugarloaf Mountain. On the 11th we went to a fish dock in Niteroi where we found two road tankers full of diesel. It was rather like being on a garage forecourt, but with two trawlers in the way. Over the next five hours we got twenty eight tonnes of fuel through a very long hose, so by 1400 we were ready to go (how many sets of wine glasses would we have got in UK for that?). We motored off out of the harbour, and anchored out in the bay to clear the water inlets. Rio harbour is not very clean; marine life must be very resilient to survive! At 1700 we up anchored and left for the open sea and the South Atlantic.

Busy hands during quiet time.

Regarding the voyage crew, with a total of twenty we were undermanned, with five in a watch and one on mess duty galley, just enough to steer and do lookout. Another problem was the steering. The hydraulics were off for a lot of the time and with about five turns of the wheel giving one degree on the rudder, the course was not exactly straight. Wind, or the lack of it, was another problem. I had looked at the routing charts for January in the South Atlantic so I didn't expect any storms, but in the following three weeks we only did a few days of real sailing, i.e. engines off. We used twenty four of those precious tonnes we had got in Rio before we got to Cape Town.

About ten days after we started off, Kyle Baker, a veteran who had been shot whilst in Afghanistan, was not well. Cape Town was contacted, and their advice was to go to Tristan da Cunha (T da C), as they had just had a resupply and had the medication required. So we headed south at full pelt. About twenty miles from T da C we were met by a RIB bearing a supply of postcards and stamps. Kyle and Tony the medic climbed aboard and were soon lost to sight. The next couple of hours were very quiet with people frantically writing postcards, 'cos we weren't going ashore.

We anchored a few hundred yards off T da C at 1900, Tony came back on board saying that Kyle would be staying until he was fit, postcards were passed over, we all got our passports back with the all important stamp in them, and at 2100 we were off again. You are only allowed ashore during the day, and, as we were expecting headwinds and being a couple of days behind schedule, any hope of a landing was off. It was very frustrating – We got the stamp in the passport, but didn't get the T-shirt! Not quite the real thing.

After that it was off to Cape Town. The headwinds were not as bad as expected, and we reached Cape Town on the Saturday evening of the 2nd February, and anchored in the bay at about 2100. It was while going into Cape Bay that we got some fairly strong winds off Table Mountain, the only decent winds in three weeks!

Well, this was not an uneventful voyage, more like a non-eventful voyage! *Lord Nelson* is due to be in the South Atlantic again next year with Captain Chris on board again. I hesitate to call another member of the PC a Jonah, but, as he said that he had been in the vicinity of T da C about five or six times and had yet to make it ashore, hmmmm....

Captain Chris.

Photo: Liz Turner

Rio de Janeiro to Cape Town by Cate Prowse

When I joined *Lord Nelson* in Rio for Leg 2, I was seventeen, I had just finished school and the airline had lost my bag. Within seconds of joining, the first person I met offered to lend me clothes. Over the next few days I learned my way around, got to know the crew and the ship, and spent hours going to and from the airport, trying to recover my bag. Captain Chris had also lost one of his, full of essential parts for the ship, and those trips out of our naval-base home were an excellent time to source other essentials.

In a tiny dive shop, Steve Higgs (Mate) used broken Spanish to explain to the Portuguese-speaking owner what he wanted. My face was used as a double for the Chief Engineer's; we were given a pink dive mask "for your daughter". I don't think the Chief was pleased. As the days waiting for bunkers dragged on, I was reunited with my bag. We went out touring, sat in the bay for New Year's Fireworks and finally left.

Rio fireworks.

Photo: Liz Turner

The challenges of Leg 2 did not end with our lack of fuel; once at sea there was a lack of wind, medical emergencies and plenty more to contend with. Perhaps because the sailing was so bad we had to find other ways to entertain ourselves. I celebrated my 18th birthday, a night of excess that was perhaps the safest way to start drinking, with less than 50m to walk to my bed. Though the voyage was just half-over I had already made such great friends, and we were more than capable of sitting in the corner of the bar and amusing ourselves for the evening. Around that day, I stayed up for twenty hours, going from a 0400 watch right through the day, and staying up for the watch after mine just to be with my friends and talk.

We celebrated Burns Night with our own 'haggis' and plenty of dressing up. A day later, I realized it was Australia Day and, as the only Aussie on board, managed to organize a game of deck cricket, with two bits of wood screwed together (and a bat painted on, so you know it's a bat), some random pieces of engineering pipe and a ball on a string. A year and a half later, deck cricket re-emerged on another voyage (both times Australia was thrashed).

When we steamed into Cape Town on the last day, I had made lifetime friends. I left the ship just a day later, promising to return when they got to Australia.

Christ the Redeemer Statue, Rio.

Deck cricket –
Cate Prowse batting.

Voyage 12 – Cape Town to Cape Town by Captain Chris Phillips

This very enjoyable short voyage saw us embark a voyage crew including a good proportion of local South Africans; some were Norton Rose employees, others had heard about us and came of their own accord. With limited options available, we sailed and motored round the Cape of Good Hope to Simonstown, where we enjoyed a night alongside in the Naval Base. We then had a good sail back round to Table Bay to anchor for the night before returning alongside in Cape Town.

Ex-Naval get together. Bosun Jim Phillips and crew members.

Approaching Table Mountain.

Photo: Alan Puddicombe

Keeping the food bill down!

Derek the cook, fish for dinner again!

On watch.

Ready for the weather.

Out on the yard.

Dates		Distances in Nautical Miles				Maximum Wind Force
Start	End	Total	Under Sail	Motor-Sailing	Motoring	
06.02.13	12.02.13	378	248	16	114	7

Wheelchair aloft, assisted by B M Ted Castledine.

Voyage 13 – Cape Town to Durban by Captain Chris Phillips

The voyage from Cape Town round to Durban once again consisted of a fair number of South Africans, as well as having a full Phillips family contingent, with my brother Jim as Bosun, and my mother and father both in the voyage crew. This could have been a tricky voyage, with the Agulhas current running down the eastern Cape coast against us, and prevailing winds also generally against our direction of travel. However, we were very lucky with the wind, and had predominantly fair breezes or calms, and made good progress around the coast, stopping in Port Elizabeth for a night and a safari arranged by two of the local VC. The ship-swallowing freak waves, which are a feature of this part of the world, were kind to us and did not make an appearance – partly because I stayed close inshore where they tend not to be!

We arrived in Durban to find a fairly underwhelming welcome compared to what we had had in Cape Town, but nonetheless we were all well looked after, and I was able to hand the ship back over to Captain Barbara and go inland to a game park to celebrate my 38th birthday.

Muster drill.

Captain Chris Phillips and dad John.

Dramatic scenery and wildlife.

... and the crew had an amzing private safari, near Port Elizabeth.

Photo: Alan Puddicombe

Photo: Mike Thomas

Photo: Alan Puddicombe

Photo: Paul Martin

Cape Town to Durban by Allen Chub

My voyage was from Cape Town to Durban in February 2013. I sailed as the Aft Port Watch Leader on this voyage of about 1,000 miles, with the Captain's parents, John Phillips (ex R.N.) and his wife Lyn on my watch.

When we arrived, Nellie (*Lord Nelson*) was moored at the Victoria and Alfred Waterfront, the centre of the action in Cape Town. Here there are lots of bars, restaurants and shops, as well as many buskers. A small group of African singers performed for us on the quayside just before we sailed, whilst well-fed seals lazed nearby in the harbour.

Musicians at the Victoria and Alfred waterfront.

On several occasions on our voyage up the coast we sailed in winds up to Force 8/9. We mainly kept close to the Wild Coast to avoid the oncoming Agulhas current and the giant freak waves it can sometimes produce, which are further offshore.

Two members of my watch were the father and son team Peter & Justin Bean, whose family emigrated from Sussex in about 1830. They own the Schotia private game reserve near Port Elizabeth, where we stopped midway for two nights. One of the highlights of our stay in Port Elizabeth was when thirty of us were guided by them around the reserve on a large open truck. This involved three separate drives as well as tea and supper around open fires. An unforgettable part of this experience was a twenty-minute meeting in the dark with a curious bull elephant, who felt with his trunk the hairs on the arms of some of our companions. As this was the start of the mating season, when the bulls' testosterone increases twenty times and they become aggressive, we spoke only in whispers and flash photography was absolutely banned.

A cannon at the game reserve is sounded every day at tea time and Liz from our watch, who has had a stroke and cannot use her right arm, was given the honour of firing it because she had climbed to the top of the foremast earlier in the day.

We set sail again, and on the final day, at about 0400 my watch, together with the on-coming watch, tacked the ship around in a fierce gale, an exhausting experience, to head for our final port of Durban.

Cape Town.

Photo: George Louw

Dates		Distances in Nautical Miles				Maximum Wind Force
Start	End	Total	Under Sail	Motor-Sailing	Motoring	
16.02.13	27.02.13	954	433	147	374	9

Photo: Paul Martin

Leg 3

Durban to Kochi by Captain Barbara Campbell

Prior to this voyage, there was concern both in the JST office and on the ship, regarding the threat of piracy. Our route would take us close to the eastern edge of the so called HRA "High Risk Area". A maritime security company called Dryad would keep us informed of any piracy activity once we were approaching the HRA. Three security guards accompanied us, joining in as Voyage Crew from Durban to Mauritius. Fortunately their services were not required and there was no known piracy or suspicious activity within 500 miles of our track. Personally I was more concerned that we would be sailing across the South Indian Ocean in cyclone season than with piracy. After voicing my concerns several times, the JST office contacted a weather-routeing company called PMTP, who would be able to monitor the whole weather systems of the Southern Ocean, and see if there was anything sinister lurking further afield than the relatively small areas of Grib weather maps that I downloaded daily via the Telaurus email system.

We departed our berth in Durban on 3rd March, and did a little 'tour' of the harbour before heading out. The evening sky was incredibly clear with the Milky Way an outstanding band across the night sky. By morning we were clear of the strong SW-running Agulhas current, but it was not until the following day that we were able to set sail. The sea was sparkling, the sun was shining, most of the crew had got over their sea-sickness and we had all the square sails set. The Spanker was added to the sail plan, so everything was flying and our speed increased to 7 knots. We furled the Royals during the evening.

In the early hours of 8th March, the wind picked up, so we furled both T'Gallants and, after a fight, brailed in the Spanker. The ship lurched around with the North winds increasing to 28 knots, gusting 35 knots. In the afternoon the ship's speed reached 10 knots. The wind showed no sign of abating as we chased eastwards, sailing close-hauled, with winds touching 45 knots.

Photo: Jono Beaty

We sailed 'full and by', under Topsails and Courses. If you want to be in big seas and feel safe, then *Lord Nelson* is a far more comfortable ride than a yacht. The wind was a force 7 or 8 all day. Various disasters befell the catering team, with fridges falling over and the vegetable locker self-destructing. I had not wanted to go as far as 33 degrees south, but we were forced to in order to find the favourable west winds. Our route took us 600 miles south of Madagascar.

An albatross graced us with an acrobatic display on Sunday 10th March; wheeling overhead, skimming low and gracefully over the seas, it was an inspiring sight. Throughout the day the wind was a light force 3 or 4 with heavy, frequent rain showers. We held a Sunday Service which was well attended. At 2200 the wind and the ship's speed started increasing relentlessly. From 8 knots, our speed increased to 9 and 10 knots in only minutes. PC and cadets were called on deck to help hand sail and we furled the T'Gallants. The wind increased further until the ship's speed reached 12.7 knots! Whilst we were handing the Main Course the wind increased to 45 knots. The rain did not let up throughout. As always, there is a really good feel factor when you are battling with sails in those conditions.

By dawn the following day the seas were big and lumpy though the wind had decreased to 18 knots. At 1100 the wind suddenly dropped and our speed fell to 0.1 knot. We started engines and handed all sails. This was an end to six days of non-stop sailing. The rain was persistent all day and the whole ship felt 'soggy'. Headwinds slowed our passage overnight.

We continued motoring on 12th March and heavy showers merged, so that it seemed the rain never stopped. Extensive yellow blotches, denoting rain, covered the radar screen. I was in daily contact with a friendly weather-man from PMPT, who was giving me weather-routeing advice. He ruined my day by telling me of a developing tropical depression 300 miles north of Mauritius. We had hoped to pick up the east winds for a fair sail to Mauritius but this depression had disrupted the usual easterly airflow.

I spent much time examining weather forecasts because it was important to make the right choice. The weather maps we received on the ship had not been reliable and we experienced much higher winds than forecast. The weather-man told me there was uncertainty about the tropical depression and whether it would develop further, but they would not know for three days. We needed to get to the west of the trough that was extending south from the tropical depression. At 1400 we altered course to a N'ly heading and at 1600 called all hands on deck for setting sails. We set all the squares except the Royals and in the ENE force 4 winds made 5 knots to the NNW. It was good to be sailing again.

The wind picked up to 30 knots in the early hours of 14th, so Marcin, 2nd Mate, handed the T'Gallants. These were reset before breakfast and we continued sailing to the west of a small area of low pressure, situated at the southern end of the trough. There was great news regarding the tropical depression; it was not developing any further and had been dropped from all the weather forecasting models. I felt much easier about it. There were sporadic showers throughout the day and the SE wind remained gusty, with the ship's speed anything from 5 to 8 knots. For the first time in five days the sky partially cleared, revealing stars in the evening sky.

Overnight we sailed round the low pressure in a clockwise direction – sailing in the Southern Hemisphere turns depressions on their heads! We set T'Gallants and Royals and started making 7 knots in a NE direction. Late morning the Fore T'Gallant ripped from head to foot near the leech. The sail was 13 years-old and had to be replaced with an overstretched 23 year-old spare, until we could reach a sail maker.

We held one of our regular security drills where all the crew mustered in the 'Citadel' which we secured in six minutes. The 'Citadel', at a minimum, consisted of the lower mess, bounded by the forward and mid-ships watertight doors, with the doors to deck also secured. We would have water, food, an iridium phone and a cramped space. The full 'citadel' was from the forward watertight doors to the aft watertight doors, incorporating the engine-room and bar in addition to the lower mess. If we were to be attacked by pirates we would need to get everyone down into the 'citadel' before a navy ship would come to our aid.

16th March – sun, blue skies, sparkling seas; we were back in the tropics after seven days of rain and gusty winds. We took advantage of the benign conditions and sent down the Fore T'Gallant sail and repaired a blown seam on the Fore Course. Crew were venturing

to lie in the sun. We held a shop and a quiz. At 2200 the wind suddenly fell away and by 2300, with no sign of a sailing wind, we clewed up sail and started engines.

Leslie with the Mauritius flag.

Photo: Karen Leverington

By dawn on 19th, the dramatic, volcanic, green island of Mauritius was becoming clearer every minute. To say the crew were excited would be an under-statement! We picked up the pilot and were berthed by 1230. The agent expedited the formalities and after lunch, most crew went ashore. The main area for cafes, bars and restaurants was the 'Waterfront' and from the gate cost £5 in a taxi, or a 30 minute walk along a busy road. Most of the crew stayed out for the evening and as the bars shut at 2200, no-one had a late night.

We took fuel first thing the following morning and the crew had the day off. Many of them hired a taxi for the day to see around Mauritius, with stops at various beaches and viewpoints. Half the population of Mauritius are of Indian origin and, outside the capital of Port Louis, Hindu temples and roadside stalls made it look like a sanitised part of India.

The morning of 21st started with assisted climbs. Fresh fruit and vegetables were delivered, and we awaited the last of our stores together with weapons for the security team. The current and wind conspired against us; it was heavy going round the north of the island with the speed down to 4 knots. We saw tropic birds and a sperm whale. Once clear of Mauritius we motored into light easterly winds. I had a busy day doing Celestial Navigation classes in the morning and sail repairing in the afternoon.

The seas decreased overnight and we started making good progress motoring. I gave another Celestial Navigation talk and sextant use – everyone who wanted to had used a sextant and brought the sun to the horizon. That afternoon I sewed the last two small patches on the Main T'Gallant sail. The evening sky was star-studded once more.

By dawn on the 24th the clear shape of the island of Rodrigues was visible. Rodrigues looked so tiny on the chart yet appeared larger than its 10 miles x 4 miles. Reefs encircled much of the island, and the access to the grandly named Port of Mathurin was blasted out of the coral reef. We anchored just outside the entrance channel, with a vertical-sided reef on either side. Immigration, Health, Customs and Coast Guard came to pay a visit. Late morning we offered the crew the chance for a swim from the ship. The water was 28 degrees and positively balmy. When everyone was back on board, we started running the crew ashore. The repaired Main T'Gallant was sent aloft and bent on. Rodrigues was quiet on a Sunday afternoon with not much to do beyond sit in a café or on a nearby beach. In the evening we had sundowners and a BBQ which went down really well in such an idyllic setting.

Cookie Dave phoning home!

Photo: Bette England

The wind was a temptress; after we weighed anchor, sails were set briefly before we had to hand them and motor. The sea temperature was 30 degrees and a glistening blue colour. The preparation of the aft deck house was completed by Bosun Oli and BMs, Stu and Jono; finally paint was being applied.

As the weather looked more promising, we started the morning of 28th with setting all sail and soon made 5 knots. We had another security drill, with all the crew going to the lower mess and the ship 'hardened'. In addition there was live firing during this drill, so that the security team could test the rifles.

30th March – overnight we had frequent gusts bringing driving rain interspersed with periods of calm. It was intensely frustrating, especially when we handed sail at 0400, only to find that the wind then became a steadier sailing wind. Sail was re-set before breakfast with a group of us working hard. After breakfast the Royals and Spanker were set to complete the sail pattern. We were soon making a good 7 knots and handed the Royals so that the ship heeled less. Heavy rain showers punctuated the day, merging into longer spells of rain. The crew complained about oilskins on and off several times a watch. Early evening we were becalmed, forcing an 'All Hands on Deck' call as we had to furl all the sails. Unfortunately a beautiful red booby, a member of the gannet family, had decided to perch on the Fore T'Gallant yard and when the Mate furled the sail, the booby's foot must have been on the furling line. With a loud indignant squawk, the booby landed on deck with a small bone broken in its foot. Rob, one of our security guards, caught the lovely creature and after a photo-shoot it was set free to continue its life circling and diving the seas.

On Easter Sunday we held a morning service by the foremast. We could see a thundery downpour to windward, but the sea was flat calm with little wind. The service started promptly and by the final hymn the wind had increased to 20 knots, with rain falling in fat drops. However, the wind soon fell light and variable again. The crew were tired, as sleep was in short supply due to the rolling. We therefore had an easy day and at 1600 held the 'Egg Drop' competition. This yielded some good eggs, destined to fly far and land safe. One was even a Dodo egg (Mauritius being the last place they lived) and there was a good twist to the story. Ian, one of the security team, launched a 'missile' and the BMs had 'Beggles'. It provided some good laughs. 'The missile' landed on the Charthouse roof, four eggs landed on deck and none were broken. As to the fifth egg… well, it may turn up on some remote island somewhere.

There was a little excitement about passing Diego Garcia the next day. In the event, the Americans extended the 3-mile restriction zone, as shown on the charts, to 10 miles. So all we saw was a low lying island to our east.

2nd April – the wind picked up overnight leaving us in no doubt that setting sails was first thing on the agenda. By 0800 the engines were off and we were sailing at 6 knots under Topsails, T'Gallants and Fore Course. In the afternoon, the wind howled and the rain blew horizontally at the crew on watch. We had gusts of wind of 35 knots and our speed reached 10.4 knots, with the ship heeling to 35 degrees. In the evening the rain was relentless.

The following day we sailed 'full and by' making our best day's noon-to-noon distance, with an average speed of 7.2 knots. Under only Topsails and Courses, close to the equator, with the wind occasionally touching 40 knots, we were having some of the best sailing of the voyage. *Lord Nelson* surged ahead, seemingly unstoppable. For the first time in days, the sky cleared a little in the afternoon.

Gusts of wind reaching 40 knots continued overnight and we enjoyed a cracking sail. Mid-morning, to the relief of Cookie Dave and Mandy, Cook's Assistant, the wind started easing. The seas were big, so to keep speed up we set the T'Gallants. Whilst the Mate was setting the Main T'Gallant, it ripped near the head. That was now five sails we had to repair, though two of them we could sew ourselves. The Bosun was keen to set the Upper Spanker, so that had an airing. Using

a sextant at noon, two VC and a cadet were within three miles of the true latitude. Three brown boobies gracefully dived and skimmed the seas, keeping the watch entertained. For the last few days we had been building up the anticipation of what was to happen to the 'pollywoggles' (those who had not crossed the line before) and several crew were apprehensive. We crossed the equator late evening, at 2319, with a number of crew getting up to witness the occasion of sailing from Southern to Northern Hemisphere.

5th April – it was a promising start for our 'Crossing the Line' ceremony. We re-set the Royals and Spanker, and Neptune's Court got ready to ascend from the depths. Neptune (Captain) and his beautiful buxom Queen (Jon, Mate) finned their way up from the depths together with Royal Surgeon, Steve, MP; Clerk of the Court, 'Sharkey' Lesley, 2nd Mate; Royal Barber Gary and Cookie Dave, Pirate Captain. The Engineers and three VC who had previously crossed the line were the Police. Many and various were the crimes of the 'pollywoggles'. Crimes ranged from putting the ship

Another 'Crossing the Equator'.

Photo: Rhi

aback, or being a Geordie, to Oli the Bosun wearing Jesus sandals, and not having the aft deck house painted in time for Neptune's arrival. All were led before the court by the police, many with their thumbs cable-tied together. They had to bow in the paddling pool, listen to their crimes, be pronounced guilty (all were guilty) and kiss Neptune's lovely fish. Oli, the cadets, the BMs and two of the Security team suffered slightly harsher treatment, in that parts of their legs or eyebrows were shaved. Everyone was fed baked beans, covered in shaving foam and slushy meringue, and had a drink syringed into their mouths. The water in the pool was filthy by the time we were only half way through, and at the end, truly foul. Mislav, in his wheelchair, was the 'rain man' who hosed everyone off as they left the pool. It was a simple, fun day and the crew then had the afternoon to wash and dry their clothes. At least the sun was back with us and the sea glistening. The wind decreased as the day carried on and late afternoon we were down to 2 knots, so handed all square sail and motored for the night. Noon: 00° 50′N 076° 57′E.

Lord Nelson 'Defence Force' in action!

Neptune must have been proud of us yesterday, for today we have blue skies and little cumulus fair-weather clouds. We set sails before breakfast, again! All day and overnight we sailed at between 3 and 5 knots. As we were well clear of the HRA we had some live practice with the rifles. It was all very carefully controlled, with an opportunity for any crew interested to have the workings of the rifles explained to them. Under the

guidance of the security team, the crew were offered the chance of firing three rounds each at a target we were towing. The target was a 25 litre drum with a lifejacket on top. Most crew took part and the security team patiently gave clear instructions. Whilst the 'target' was being hoisted back on to the stern platform, the line attaching it to the ship parted, the drum being thoroughly waterlogged. I instantly imagined a ship finding this drum with a bullet-ridden *Lord Nelson* lifejacket on it, so we had a completely unannounced man overboard drill and the target was recovered by the DOTI boat crew in nine minutes. Not bad for being unannounced and with the ship sailing at 5 knots.

Our ETA at the floating weapons installation off Galle was 0730 on 8th April. The weapons were checked out and disembarked. We continued on to Galle and made our way between the fort and the point with a Buddhist shrine. The harbour was small but ideal, and we were all fast alongside our berth on Closenburg Pier at 1030. The crew set off to Galle Fort, which they really enjoyed. Some spent the evening there, watching the sun set and having a meal; others got a tuk-tuk to Unawatuna, a slightly hippy, laid back and quiet area with restaurants along the beach, where a meal and several beers cost under a fiver.

The following day the crew had an early start for a coach tour departing at 0630. They went to a tea plantation and factory, followed by a safari at Udawelaway. Wild elephants in abundance came close; they also saw crocodiles, water buffalo and innumerable exotic birds. Sri Lanka was a huge hit with the crew, and many vowed to come back on holiday.

Prior to our arrival in India, most spare hands helped the BMs use 'Metal Brite' to temporarily get rid of the rust streaks which stained our bulwarks. They did a brilliant job, which was good as the Indian Navy might well have cast a critical eye over the state of *Lord Nelson*. We continued preparing the ship and getting her tidy for the photo shoot on 13th. In the afternoon the repaired Main T'Gallant was bent on, giving us a complete set of sails.

We arrived at the Rendezvous with sister ships *Tarangini* and *Sudarshini* at 0630 on 13th April, and started setting sails soon after. I am not boasting, but our sails were beautifully set, while theirs were hung on their buntlines, on the forward braces or on a stay. We launched our DOTI boat to take photos, and the aerial photography from the helicopter, which flew around for a full hour, provided plenty of shots, including an excellent one of the three sister ships, which was used in the local paper. We handed sails and motored to Kochi, 20 miles away. On passage the sails were stowed and the pilot, along with our main man in India, Soli, boarded. *Tarangini* went ahead of us with *Sudarshini* astern as we passed Fort Kochi and the Chinese fishing nets. Stuart, BM, and Joyce were unfortunately not allowed ashore as they had neither visa nor Discharge Book. Many of the crew went to the Colonial Malabar Hotel for a meal.

Keeping a good lookout.

The following morning most crew went on a houseboat into the backwaters; others explored Fort Kochi while the PC did some essential maintenance jobs. In the evening we all went to a restaurant called the Ginger House. It had a great location by the river and luckily they opened in the evening just for us. One of the cadets had her 18th birthday and a good last night meal was enjoyed by all.

15th April – another early start for the Captain as the Immigration official needed to see the off-going crew who were bound for the airport at 0600.

Joyce, who had been in floods of tears for three days as she could not get ashore, was denied a transit visa, despite the agents being confident that she would get one. We desperately tried to get her an emergency visa, without success, meaning that unfortunately the only parts of Kerala that Joyce saw were the fishing boats and daily life on the river, where we were moored, and what she saw from a taxi on her way to the airport.

With excellent camaraderie, great fun, plenty of sail handling and exhilarating sailing, a great voyage was enjoyed by all.

Photo: Lee Wells

Never Look down!

Photo: Jono Beaty

Dates		Distances in Nautical Miles				Maximum Wind Force
Start	End	Total	Under Sail	Motor-Sailing	Motoring	
28.02.13	15.04.13	4851	2235	2022	594	9

Voyage 14 – Kochi to Kochi by Captain Chris Phillips

Our experience in India was made considerably easier by the assistance of the Indian Navy, through the Trust's Sail Training International contact, Captain Soli Contractor. In fact, without the wholehearted and unstinting support of the Navy, Voyage 14 would never have happened. The other Indian authorities, in particular the immigration authorities, having learnt their particularly obtuse bureaucracy during the days of the Raj, were evidently unwilling to give it up or bend the rules for this strange ship which had turned up. We didn't fit neatly into any of their categories: we were not a yacht, neither were we a passenger vessel; we were not a cargo ship, despite being classified as such on our certificates, and we were certainly not a warship like the Indian Navy's two sister ships to *Lord Nelson*, the *INS Sudarshini* and *Tarangini*. Yachting is virtually unknown on the subcontinent; everyone is either too busy making money or simply surviving, so the concept of a ship full of people who had paid to work on board her was too much for them to comprehend.

Indian Naval cadets paid us a visit.

Photo: Brian Norrey

As a result we were severely restricted in what we could do during this week-long voyage on the Keralan coast, due to an unwillingness for us to trade in Indian waters. The Navy saved the day by vouching for us and inviting us to visit their Ezhimala naval academy about 150 miles up the coast at Mount Dilli. Even so, when we made our departure from Kochi on 19th April, we were officially proceeding out to the anchorage outside the port, but when we had dropped off the pilot, we turned right and none-too-stealthily headed NW up the coast. Unfortunately the winds in this part of the world are predominantly NW'ly, so we motored all the way to our destination, remaining inside the 12-mile limit so as not to stray into the HRA for piracy, thus annulling our insurance. Instead we had to weave our way between hundreds of poorly-lit fishing boats!

Ann embarking the tender.

Photo: Brian Norrey

We anchored in a fairly exposed anchorage under Mount Dilli, and enjoyed a musical soiree on board that evening. The following day we received a visit from naval cadets in the morning, who came on board in a locally-hired fishing skiff. This vessel returned ashore with the first load of *Lord Nelson's* crew, including myself, all done up in tropical whites, for a return visit to the Academy. This was one of the most incredible boat rides I have ever had, with the skiff's coxswain skilfully negotiating the skiff through the breaking seas over a sand bar before entering a shallow creek, where we landed and were taken by bus to the Academy. Strangely for such an establishment, there is no direct access to the sea from the college; they do all their boat handling training on an adjacent lagoon. Eventually all the crew were landed and bussed to the Academy. In the meantime I had gone on ahead to meet the Commandant, Vice Admiral Chauhan, for a chat and Chai. The crew were treated to a tour of the Academy's facilities, not made easy for our wheelchair users by the fact that the architect of this new establishment obviously had a thing for steps, and had not heard of accessibility! After our tour and a substantial curry lunch in the gunroom, we were ferried back to the creek and had an equally exciting trip back out to the ship in the same skiff.

After a second night at anchor we set sail the following day and headed back down the coast, under sail this time, arriving back in Kochi in good time to wave our VC goodbye.

Kochi to Kochi by Sue Tupper Watch Leader

The Kochi voyage was wonderful, warm and a movie montage. Think "Life of Pi", James Bond, Tom Cruise (Top Gun) and Tom Hanks (Captain Phillips). Having enjoyed and weathered the maiden Leg 1 to Rio voyage, I hadn't necessarily expected (but had secretly hoped) to be doing another Sail the World voyage, but the India one called to me and became one of my top ten voyages ever. Indian authorities go a tad over the top in visa paperwork which sadly meant that our Open Ship to welcome potential Indian sailors on board was scuppered, and in order to fill bunks we had a few last minute crew join from the local shipping agents who were kind, friendly, warm and helpful.

Amongst our voyage crew we were lucky enough to have Soli, a retired Indian naval captain, and he negotiated for us to visit the Indian naval academy north of Kochi, which ended up being our voyage destination up the coastline and back. An old blue painted boat just like that in the "Life of Pi" film ferried us ashore from the ship at anchor to visit the naval academy, surfing waves towards palm tree-lined backwaters. Bemused uniformed cadets in white shorts, shirts and long black knee socks welcomed us to their academy buildings which resembled a baddie's lair from a James Bond film. The building was not designed for disabled visitors, so Ann was delighted to be carried by six uniformed "Top Gun" style cadets up and down the wide flights of stairs before we scruffy tall ship sailors were waited on at a silver service lunch of delicious Keralan curry. Like any other JST voyage, you just never know what is going to happen, and this was yet another bizarre but beautiful intermingling of kind international humanity.

The Naval 'Gun Room' where we ate delicious curries.
Photo: Chikako Yamamoto

Captain Phillips.

Brian Norrey

As usual, our ship attracted interest from local sailors, but the ones on this voyage were just like those on the Captain Phillips film with Tom Hanks, which had just been in cinemas in the UK, but what looked like pirates trying to board the ship were, in fact, local fishermen trying to sell their catch. After lengthy haggling by our Indian voyage crew the fish and squid were eventually bought and expertly prepared by cookie Derek.

The return sail back to Kochi involved some wonderful sailing in warm seas and light winds, captured by Andy and Jimmy who were on board as official photographers, so many of the sunny images and videos on the JST website and brochures were taken on that voyage.

Photo: Sue Tupper

Photo: Chikako Yamamoto

Local fishermen.

Photo: Mike Drummond Smith

Dates		Distances in Nautical Miles				Maximum Wind Force
Start	End	Total	Under Sail	Motor-Sailing	Motoring	
18.04.13	24.04.13	307	124	0	183	4

Photo: Chikako Yamamoto

Leg 4

Kochi to Singapore by Captain Chris Phillips

Having worked out the system in the previous week, our departure from Kochi second time around was far less painful; again we received much-needed assistance from the Indian Navy, Soli Contractor, and our agents Mr Jolly and Ronak Shetty. My most memorable moment from the stay in Kochi was going with Derek the cook, Ronak and Mr Jolly to a local hypermarket (newly opened) to buy stores, and watching £1600 worth of food going through the till. This was followed by a novel visit to McDonalds, where there was not a red meat product in sight.

The day came for our departure, and we were seen off by the Indian Navy's yacht *Mhadei*, which had recently returned from its second single-handed circumnavigation. However, Kochi was not giving us up that easily, and just outside the port we had to anchor and get divers in to clear our seawater intakes, which had finally succumbed to the rich soup of detritus which floated in the harbour there. Our diver was a volunteer, Cdr Dilip Donde, who had been the skipper of Mhadei for one of her circumnavigations;

after a few minutes in the water the intakes were clear and we gave him a bottle of Single Malt for his trouble. We were now free to get underway and head to the SE for our first port of Galle, in Sri Lanka.

This had been a port of call on the way into Kochi, and was where the ship had disembarked the security team and their weapons prior to arrival in India after crossing the Indian Ocean. As a result, the agent there knew us well and was able to make arrangements fairly easily for us, with the requisite number of cigarettes and bottles of whisky (Indian) changing hands. Whilst we were alongside there I was able to get a fuller picture of the development of two cyclones in the Bay of Bengal, one either side of the equator, which would have an important bearing on my passage plan across to the Malacca Straits.

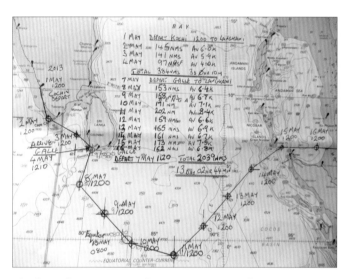

The lengths some people go to, to cross the equator!
Photo: Carolyn Broughton

I delayed departure from Galle by 24 hours to allow the storms to get well ahead of us (I didn't want to run into the back of either of them), and then we set off down towards the equator, where it looked as though we would avoid both of them. Due to the weakness of the Coriolis effect at the equator, tropical revolving storms are physically unable to get within about 15 degrees latitude of them, leaving us a nice corridor to squeeze through. This route would, of course, add a considerable distance to our voyage – about 500 miles – but would be much safer, and would also add a

further two equator crossings to the four already in the Sail the World programme – something about which I was particularly pleased, because up until then, they had all been in Barbara's voyages!

Whilst we avoided the cyclones successfully, we experienced very squally conditions all the way across the Bay, with incredibly heavy rain showers and short, sharp increases in the wind strength, sometimes from nothing to gale force in moments. It was one of these squalls which finally killed the roller furling gear in the Fore T'Gallant yard after 28 years of operation. The foil to which the sail is attached, and which normally remains inside the yard, pulled out through the slot and would not go back in. It was partly the damage sustained when this happened, and partly the damage from the attempts to force it back into the yard, which meant that the gear was no longer usable (and the supply of spares for this one-off, obsolete system had long since run out). For this voyage, it meant that effectively we were without a Fore T'Gallant.

Cable car, Langkawi.

We arrived in Langkawi, a beautiful island in northern Malaysia, on the 17th May, and enjoyed a good couple of days alongside there in the yacht club marina, before we embarked on the next stage of the voyage, down the Straits of Malacca. These Straits were formerly notorious for piracy, but a combination of the death penalty being introduced in Malaysia for piracy, and the destruction of the main base for the pirates during the 2004 Tsunami, meant that the risk was considerably reduced. That said, we still had our wits about us and had to consider that there was still a possibility that some opportunistic Indonesian fisherman in a fast boat might consider us easy prey. As it happened, of course, the passage passed off without incident, and without any sailing either, as the weather was predominantly calm (and oppressively hot) for the entire passage down the Straits and into the Singapore Strait.

Yet another Birthday!

Photo: Terry Coultard

Lord Nelson alongside, at night.

Photo: Max Mudie

We finally arrived in Singapore on the 22nd May, and, after anchoring in the quarantine anchorage to clear the ship in, we proceeded into our berth in Cruise Bay, right next to a very high-profile shopping centre called Vivocity. This berth not being part of the port infrastructure, the authorities felt it necessary to make our gangway a point of entry in and out of the country, so for our whole stay alongside we had armed guards and an x-ray body scanner and baggage scanner at the gangway.

Photo: Ryan Shore

Whilst the voyage finished here, the crew were well entertained in Singapore, with various sponsors looking after us, including Norton Rose and a rival law firm, Holman Fenwick holding events on board and ashore. On one evening, the entire permanent crew decamped to the British High Commission for a party thrown jointly by His Excellency himself and Norton Rose.

Dates		Distances in Nautical Miles				Maximum Wind Force
Start	End	Total	Under Sail	Motor-Sailing	Motoring	
28.04.13	25.05.13	2503	1105	810	588	8

Kochi to Singapore by Lucilla Phelps

I arrived early in Kochi to have time to explore this amazing part of India before setting sail on *Lord Nelson*. Kerala is supposedly the most educated part of the country. I had been advised to stay in Fort Kochi, which I did, and loved the area and the proximity to everything, especially the famed Chinese fishing nets, one of the photographic highlights of my stay.

Chinese fishing nets, Kochi.

Photo: Lucilla Phelps

Firstly came the nightmare which is Indian bureaucracy. When asked for the reason for your visit to India, "To Crew a Tall Ship" is not the usual tourist reply and the resulting paperwork involved was unexpected and unwelcome. Once on board *Lord Nelson*, however, it was the usual mix of meeting the other voyage crew and getting to know our watch. My buddy was Ann, a wheelchair user, who has been a good friend since we sailed together in 2000. We have sailed together many times since.

Once we were on our way and sailing south, keeping to Indian shipping lines due to the possibility of pirates, we had a marvellous time with most sails set in sun and warmth. We had practised the lockdown in case we were boarded, but in the event nothing untoward happened. Due to a cyclone in the northern hemisphere and also in the southern hemisphere, it was decided to sail south and cross the equator, which

meant we had to miss going to Phuket and Penang. Instead we altered course and landed in the Langkawi Islands (shades of James Bond movies where some were filmed), which were very beautiful. The captain, Chris, did a stern mooring to a pontoon, which was very impressive. We then sailed down the Malacca Straits towards Singapore; a very congested waterway but we managed a good sail, despite the shipping traffic. Our final destination was Singapore, where there was open ship and lots to do. The metro system is magnificent and so wheelchair-friendly that Ann and I managed to get around easily.

Beautiful Kochi sunset.

Photo: Lucilla Phelps

Of course the sailing was wonderful, the sights breathtaking but the thing that always remains is the mix of people and the other crew members. Friends for the journey; inspiring people with differing disabilities and fascinating stories. One such chap was a soldier, Dave Hart, wounded in Afghanistan, where he had had his arms almost blown off. After scores of operations and thanks to his willpower, he can use one arm which is nearly OK and one which he uses like a hook. The photograph shows when he climbed up the ratlines and got on to the course yard next to me. I was telling him about how we do a harbour stow. He managed so well and said at the end "I never thought I could do this". Sailing has inspired him now to undertake some more training and run a marathon. What a fellow! The image shows very well the joy on his face and on mine as I was so pleased for him.

Roll on the next trip with the JST that we all support.

Hanging around, Lucilla Phelps and Dave Hart.
Photo: Carolyn Broughton

Kochi to Singapore by Dr Louise Crockett

No ordinary ship, no average voyage

The Jubilee Sailing Trust's *Lord Nelson* is a barque of fifty-five metres; 498 tonnes of beautiful three-masted square-rigged ship, circumnavigating the globe for the first time. She is a symphony of line and sail.

The JST is a charity taking able and disabled people as voyage crew. Sailing with JST cuts away prejudice, and challenges our fears, for Nellie takes no passengers. We help each other across the ocean. The voyagers are divided into four "watches" of mixed ability and aptitude. Each watch takes turn to run the ship, on helm, compass steering, raising and handing sail, keeping lookout. Off watch there's plenty to do; eating often, sleeping sometimes, "Happy Hour" daily. This is kept secret until the crew have signed on; it's when we clean the ship from deck to heads. Taking it all in, the swells, the sails, the ship, it takes all day.

The long night watches are times to discover your fellow crew. We are 36 in company: injured soldiers from the latest Afghan war, two wheelchair users, three men who are blind and deaf, people with bionic joints, diabetics, people with MS, cerebral palsy, neurological disorders. Some disablement was self-evident, some hidden, but we all had some learning to do. Making

all this work is the "permanent" crew of professionals: the captain and deck officers, engineers, medics, cooks, and bosun's mates. They navigate the ocean, and tell us which of the 50 miles of rope to pull and when (did I mention the ship has no winches?), how to prepare a jack-fruit and brace the yards. We learned the language of Nelson's Navy, at least the polite bits.

The *Lord Nelson* was purpose-built in 1986 for a mixed-ability crew, with lifts between decks, grab-rails, tactile guides to deck position, audio compass, and cleats for securing wheelchairs on rolling decks. Below there are bunks with some privacy for wheelchair space, "cabins", close to disabled facilities. The rest of the crew live in cupboards in the fo'c'sle. A Buddy system operates, and we learned to help when asked.

Going up the ratlines, up the mast, secured by harness, is voluntary. Some disabled people were helped aloft by the rest of us. Anne, a crew member in a wheelchair and a lawyer in "real life", tried out new self-lifting gadgets to haul herself to the futtocks. Her smile says it all - "Yes I can!" We are all lifted by her courage.

Tony is unforgettable. He is blind and deaf, and relies on hearing aids, touch, proprioception, and his memory to find his way. And friendships. He taught us how to "guide"; with his hand on your elbow or shoulder, he can tell your direction. We chat long into the pre-dawn watch. He has learned not to be afraid. Fear drives us to safety, but is our gaoler. Tony is a free man.

We sail our ship from hot, humid, thunderstruck Kochi (bottom left of India) through monsoon lightning drama to Sri Lanka, a gentler-seeming island. We dock in Galle, a UNESCO site for its Dutch colonial architecture and hugely thick garrison walls. These centuries-old walls saved the old town from the tsunami. Road-side graves made that history real all along the coast.

Our voyage was due to be east to the Great Channel north of Sumatra, into the Molucca straits and south to Singapore. But a tropical revolving storm developed - sufficient to rip canvas and damage limbs, if not lives. It was heading our way from the south-east. Circumavigating the danger took twelve days and two Equator crossings, not five days of the rhumb-line voyage.

We ran up "sailor strainers" (metre high nets atop the side rail, between standing rigging) to catch crew being thrown from the deck. Comforting! There was a 3-4 metre swell on the storm's edge, and trotting white horses on top. Oh, how we sailed! A beautiful movement. Rising over blue walls of water that came on in rhythm, our Nellie rolled 40 degrees to port, then to starboard, for days. Routines on board became increasingly crazy. Dressing, showering, eating meals when rolling sideways is interesting, and we all grew bruises. It took me four days to balance free and upright. The blind guys found it easy.

In long passages, days merge as one. A timelessness develops, at least among the crew. The officers have satnav and electronic plotting to mark the passage of space-time. But the crew live in a continuum of now. The world looks the same, the days feel the same. The nights are fabulous under new stars (oh, the feel of warm wind caressing bare arms!) or sometimes sudden monsoon drenching.

After seven (or maybe seventeen?) days of watching, we grow desperate to see something. Anything. Deep-sea, the ocean surface seems empty of life. A dolphin sighting, or a passing determined turtle brings a relay call from bowsprit to bridge, and a buzz about the ship again.

We land for supplies at Langkawi, a tropical paradise island, built of Karst, so the leaflets said. Ashore, we explore. No tides mean no foreshore. The narrow beaches are backed by mangrove swamp, plantations or veranda-ed houses, only the sea is blue like ours.

Heading south between Straits settlements, Malay pirates on proahs, VOC and British East India Company towards Raffles' Singapore, we enter the busiest shipping channel in the world, and sail into the 21st century. Reckless burning has set Sumatra on fire. The watched waters become dotted with careless plastic - a bottle, a flip-flop, civilisation's detritus. We sail to our berth in the heart of the city, close to Sentosa Island, the ultimate meta-theme park. Singapore has money and buildings to impress, a metro system to covet, but no sense of history.

We have lived aboard in close company, have become a team. We've grown proud of our ship, of each other, and of our personal voyages of discovery.

Since 1986 *Lord Nelson* has taken over 24,000 people sailing, 10,000 of whom were physically disabled, and nearly 5,000 were in wheelchairs. Do you want to be part of her future?

Dave Hart assisted climb.
Photo: Lucilla Phelps

Voyage 15 – Singapore to Singapore by Captain Chris Phillips

Another short local voyage, and we embarked a healthy number of Singaporeans and Indonesian VC, for what promised to be a very different voyage.

We sailed from Singapore with few complications – although we had to go out to anchor in order to take our duty-free stores and to clear out. Once this was completed, we had to negotiate the incredibly busy traffic schemes which abound through the Singapore Straits. This, of course, could not really be done under sail, so we motored out to the east and then NE to aim for Tioman Island on the east coast of Malaysia – an area, incidentally, in which there have been a number of piracy attacks since our visit.

The intention was to motor to the north of Tioman and then set sail back to the south to anchor, but obviously the wind had not been told about this and failed to do the job, so much of the passage was under power.

In the early evening of 30th May, we anchored off the administrative centre of the island at Telek Tukuk, and enjoyed a pleasant tropical evening at anchor before getting clearance the following morning to go ashore and explore.

After a barbecue on board and a second night at anchor, we cleared out and weighed anchor to head back to Singapore, unfortunately with a complete lack of useable wind. We spent the time on passage stowing the square sails, then weaving our way back through the Singapore Straits traffic schemes into the clearance anchorage prior to our arrival back alongside on the 3rd June.

Dates		Distances in Nautical Miles				Maximum Wind Force
Start	End	Total	Under Sail	Motor-Sailing	Motoring	
28.05.13	03.06.13	412	13	18	381	4

Singapore to Singapore by Jon and Caroline Button

This 7-day voyage gave us the chance to sail in warm Asian waters for the first time. We spent three days in Singapore before the voyage, acclimatising ourselves to the heat and humidity, and also trying to get over the jet lag. Singapore is a lovely place, with lots to do and see. We hired mobility scooters to get around, which worked brilliantly. The easiest way to get around is via the linked, underground shopping malls – they provide the comfort of air conditioning, and also avoid the minefield of trying to find pavements with dropped kerbs. The MRT, the spotlessly clean and punctual underground transport service, was totally accessible to us as well.

The voyage crew had been boosted by a large number of late recruits from the open ship the previous weekend. We had a mix of Singaporeans, Malaysians, two from Hong Kong, plus a good sprinkling of those of us who had flown in from the UK.

Nellie was moored up outside Vivo City, a large new shopping mall on the waterfront, opposite Sentosa Island. She looked magnificent, as always. Soon after leaving port, we had to anchor in the harbour to take on the all important booze supplies as we were not allowed to load those while docked. Also immigration had to come aboard to stamp our passports. We were soon on our way again, dodging the many tankers and container ships entering or leaving Singapore, one of the busiest ports in the world. One ship had obviously shed some of its load, and we had to take care not to run into floating planks of wood and even a couple of floating palm trees!

Once out of the busy shipping channels, we were able to do the usual evacuation drills, learn how to brace yards and set sail, and hands aloft. Captain Chris had decided that we would go up the east coast of Malaysia, as it was likely to be much quieter than the Malacca Straits on the west coast. Although we were now experts with the sails, there was a slight technical hitch – no wind. This area is known as the Doldrums, because there is very rarely much wind. I think in the whole week we only sailed 11 miles totally under sail – the rest of the time we used the motors.

Our destination was Tioman, a small idyllic holiday island. It is the island where Ursula Andress came out of the water in the James Bond film Dr. No. We anchored off there in the late afternoon, then the next morning the DOTI boat was used to ferry us ashore. The Malaysian coastguard decided that they wanted to show off their powerful speed boat, so intercepted the DOTI boat. They claimed there were too many people in wheelchairs on the boat (there were two). Now, the JST has been doing this for many years, so they certainly know what is a safe load. After a bit of discussion we were allowed to carry on. I'm sure the coastguards had never seen anything like it! The island was beautiful, not very busy at all. We set off in groups – some heading for the snorkelling beach, some to sit on the beach all day, others to explore the culinary delights and the duty free shop. We had a lovely lunch in a local restaurant/shack, then went to the beach and swam in the sea. At the end of the day we had a barbecue on board, looking out at the island bathed in the setting sun.

On our watch we had Joseph from Hong Kong, who is totally blind. He epitomised the ethos of the JST – he got stuck into absolutely everything, from helming, coiling ropes, mess duty to happy hour. He will be dining out on stories of his voyage for years to come. Also on board was Jovin Tan, who has represented Singapore in the last three Paralympics at sailing. Everyone got on really well, and some lasting friendships were made. After the excitement of Tioman, we motored back to Singapore. Going through the shipping lanes at night, with all the sailing vessels alongside us was quite a sight. We had to anchor again for immigration formalities, then it was back to Vivo City and the end of the voyage.

Leg 5

Singapore to Fremantle by Captain Barbara Campbell

The VC joined the ship which was berthed by the bustling waterfront shopping complex of Vivo-City. The following morning started with Happy Hour, followed by Hands Aloft and Bracing practice. Once this had finished, the VC were free to wander around.

The van delivering food stores had to be off the complex by 0700 the following morning. Stores were booked for 0500 and many of the VC turned out to help the PC and volunteers. We did well and by 0615 we had all

the stores onboard. The heavens then opened, leaving us feeling smug that we had taken on stores early. The crew were free for the remainder of the day. Many went to Sentosa Island, others to China Town, the Raffles Hotel or the shops; all had a good time.

The pilot boarded at 0930 on 10th June and we were soon bound for West Jurong anchorage, for immigration, taking on fuel bunkers, fresh water and duty free. We then had a delay while we waited

Heading aloft to stow sails at sea.

Photo: Laura Blackburn

for a pilot, who finally boarded at 1915. My hope of transiting the Singapore Straits by midnight did not happen. Luckily we had no rain and enjoyed good visibility with well-behaved traffic.

We rounded Horsburgh Light as dawn broke and turned to the east, to clear the Singapore Straits, before entering the South China Sea. Surprisingly, we had a sailing wind and set Topsails, Main T'Gallant and Fore Course before turning the engines off for a few hours. At 2000 we handed sail as the wind fell light.

At 0354 on 12th we crossed the equator amidst heavy showers. The day brightened, and at lunchtime we went ahead with the fun of the Crossing the Line Ceremony. Neptune and his Court, in all their finery, ascended from the depths. The 'pollywoggles' (all those who had not yet crossed the line and paid their respects to Neptune), were gathered by the police and forced to kneel before Neptune and his wife. Their crimes were read out and funnily enough, all were guilty! Kneeling in the pool, they 'kissed the fish' and received their 'medicine' and tablets. Needless to say the medicine and tablets (baked beans) were clumsily administered by the surgeon, ending up all over the place. Those pollywoggles with serious crimes (the cadets and the BMs) would have an occasional shaved eyebrow. The two last pollywoggles to be tried were Dan, Cook's Assistant, with his girlfriend Anna. Dan chose the

moment to propose to Anna. Once again, it was a fun day and much appreciated by the crew. Noon: 00° 32′S 106° 47′E Wind SE 1-2

Very 'Amateur Dramatics'.

13th June was our first beautiful sunny day at sea. Smoko featured a cake for Dan and Anna, which was followed by a fire drill for the permanent crew. At 1800 we altered course in Selat Karimata. Leaving the South China Sea, we entered the Java Sea with our speed reduced due to the adverse current. On the trip from India to Singapore, the foil inside the Fore T'Gallant yard had been badly damaged and was unusable. The only way of setting a T'Gallant on that yard was to convert a 23 year-old spare T'Gallant sail, from a roller furling sail to a traditional sail. The Bosun and I had been busy sewing reinforced patches on the old sail to take grommets for the buntlines. There was a fair bit of work to do, but it passed many pleasant afternoons.

Despite motoring there was plenty to do, with a talk by our two blind crew members on blind and deaf awareness. There was a competition to see which watch could make the most baggywrinkle, resulting in the bridge being adorned with lengths of baggywrinkle. Oli and I had started stitching grommets onto the reinforced patches on the Fore T'Gallant sail. Various crew members were going higher up the mast each day; this activity was followed by a quiz in the evening.

Cheery Chipps heading for the fire drill, second engineer Paul Cole.

Photo: Laura Blackburn

We held a well attended Sunday Service by the foremast when Margaret, CA, displayed her hidden talent by playing the violin for us. We set sail and remained under sail until 1700, the wind a SE force 2 to 3.

17th June – At 0730 we passed through the Kamudi Islands, leaving the Java Sea behind and entering the Bali Sea. Yet again we were able to set sail in light winds for the day. On our way to Bali we set sail four times but only managed to cover 60 miles under sail. In the evening we were in the grip of a 4 knot current that sweeps south. We remained in this current until we reached Benoa, Bali. Slowing down in the strong current was not easy. A large cruise ship at anchor probably contributed to the chaos inside the harbour. Think unregulated Cowes week with speed boats towing large inflatable mattresses. The thought that we did not have a Risk Assessment for an inflatable mattress wrapped round a yard entered my head! As we could not see our berth, I sent the DOTI boat in

early. Oli, the Bosun, reported that the berth did not look long enough for us to go in bow first as we had been instructed to. I decided to do a Mediterranean Moor and go in stern-first between a mega yacht and the finger berth. The bow overhung the berth by over 15 metres. With a little cross current it was not an easy manoeuvre. The JST got their money's worth out of me for getting us alongside. Once there our very friendly agents, two Irish brothers and a Scotsman from Indo Yacht Support (IYS), helped us through the paperwork maze. The crew were given shore leave and most found an ATM on the way to a restaurant or bar.

Following the voyage photo next morning, we organised taxi tours for the VC. These were fantastic value at £35, plus a tip, for a taxi with a driver-guide for eight hours. The crew all went to a temple by the Ocean, which they thought spectacular, before heading to the cool of the hills to see the iconic views of terraced rice paddies. Most crew then hit the beaches whilst some continued inland. In the evening we co-hosted a reception with the Royal Bali Yacht Club. We had Balinese dancers in traditional bright coloured dress and make-up from an orphanage for street children. They performed really well and were pleased with the donations. The wife of the Commodore of the Yacht Club cooked a traditional Balinese meal for 46 crew and 50 guests; the ship provided sundowners, music and dessert. From small beginnings the reception turned into a real party, much aided by our Irish and Scottish friends at IYS.

Balinese dancers after their performance by the ship.

Our stop in Bali ended all too soon. Using the anchor to pull us ahead, we crept out of the berth. Again it was mayhem in the harbour with all sorts of speed boats criss-crossing our path. Once clear, we motored south west and set all square sail, including our modified Fore T'Gallant which the Bosun, myself and Bosun's Mates had finished sewing and bent on aloft. The sail was 23 years old, fragile and owed us nothing. The sail itself set beautifully, so we were justifiably proud! For the first time this voyage the VC encountered an ocean swell. Many had forgotten what it was like to be on a moving ocean as hitherto the sea had been so quiet. For several days we had been plotting a trough of low pressure which had brought unseasonal bad weather to Christmas Island. Ships had not been allowed into the bay which is very exposed to the NW swell.

22nd June – The ship continued to roll, providing interesting moments for all the crew, especially those in wheelchairs or those trying to keep food on plates. A local fishing boat came close, holding up a big fish. Clearly they were asking if we wanted it. The answer was yes, as we still had not caught a thing on our own lines! Language was a problem. However "actions speak louder than words" and for a bottle of cheap Indian whisky, the crew of the boat threw over two barracuda from a distance of 3 metres. Oli bravely caught the first big barracuda; either that or he was standing in the wrong place! Then the fishermen threw four small tuna plus another barracuda. We reciprocated by giving them the equivalent of £12, all our remaining coins from Bali. It was a lot of fish for a small amount of money, but the fishermen were pleased. I made sushi for everyone before giving the first of my Celestial Navigation and sextant talks. Whilst the crew were eating sushi by the mainmast, I told them that after consultation with the Harbour Master of Christmas Island we had decided not to call there but to continue onto Cocos Keeling Island. Under all square sail, the speed gradually increased from 4 to 6 knots. The forecast showed the wind backing into the NW but we took a chance and sailed overnight. Squalls at 2300 saw us handing the Royals and Fore T'Gallant.

In the early hours of the 24th our speed reached 9.3 knots in a gust. However, when the wind moderated, the speed was not enough to overcome the swell, so we rolled heavily at times. We were able to remain sailing until after morning smoko, as the wind continually backed into the NW. A red-footed booby was back on the Fore T'Gallant yard – this appears to be a favourite perch for these beautiful sea birds. At 1600 I gave the second of the Celestial Navigation talks. I had been concerned quite how I was going to explain the use of a sextant to our two blind crew, but they were both simply amazing and handled the sextants well, albeit they could not see the sun.

Red footed Booby on the spanker boom.

25th June – As forecast, the wind backed from NW to west and to the south overnight. Straight after the morning meeting we set sail. In a SE wind, force 3 to 4, we made 4.5 knots, just right for the Big Egg Drop competition. For the first time in memory, not a single egg made it to deck intact. Three went over the side, one having an unfortunate bounce off a fender; the two that landed on deck were both broken. Still, it provided some laughs. The afternoon and evening were very pleasant, the ship sailing easily with little motion on a balmy night.

After a quiet night under sail, the wind increased to 20 knots. The Courses were clewed up as we had to arrive at Cocos Keeling during daylight. The wind was gusting 35 knots at times, causing us to heel 38 degrees to starboard. Extra safety ropes and the 'sailor strainer' netting were rigged. VC who were wobbly on their feet had to remain below decks. Apart from the mid-ships area, the decks were out of bounds due to the angle of heel and the slipperiness of the decks. Huge slaps of water hit the ship's side, making a bang that one of the VC described as 'like a cannon going off'.

Another sleepless night ensued, with the ship rolling up to 38 degrees to starboard and 30 degrees to port. At 0830 we clewed up the Main Topsail and Mizzen Staysail in an attempt to reduce speed below 6 knots. The wind remained a steady SE 25 knots with moderate to rough seas. Food and drink ended up on the decks despite the best of efforts. At noon, despite the roll, all five Noon sights were within four miles of the correct latitude. Under just Outer Jib and Fore Topsail we made 6.5 knots. We appeared to be going faster and faster. The west-going current did not help. In desperation to slow down, we also furled the Outer Jib, leaving us under Fore Topsail alone.

Huge tides and cross-currents at the entrance to Cocos Keeling meant that we were steering up to 50 degrees off the course we were trying to make. Entering a Coral atoll, where everything is blue sea fringed with low-lying islands, and where hidden reefs marked by tiny beacons lurk beneath the surface, is not something you get to do every day. We were the largest vessel to have

Paradise on Cocos Island, *Lord Nelson* anchored in the background.

visited Cocos Keeling in two years. In the afternoon we had a much-needed quiet time, as it was the first time the ship had been relatively still for a few days. The Bosun and I spent the afternoon aloft doing sail repairs. The VC slept, lazed on deck or fished. Paul the cadet caught three reef sharks which were subsequently thrown back in. We had sundowners in the evening followed by dinner on deck.

Cadet Paul had an unexpected nibble on his finger.

30th June – Cocos Keeling is a typical Indian Ocean atoll and we were anchored right inside it! We ran the crew ashore to Direction Island for the day while a late morning boat took some of the PC and volunteers, with packed lunches for all. The DOTI boat trips were extremely wet as the sea was bouncy and waves broke over the boat. Direction Island was untouched and it was a treat and a privilege to go there. Walking along the beach, swimming or snorkelling the 'Rip' were all wonderful. The 'Rip' was where the sea had carved a narrow gulley in the reef. The sea ran through at 4 to 6 knots. You jumped in where you felt comfortable with the strength of the water, and then drifted with the flow. There below, as you were swept along, were giant grouper, parrot fish, reef sharks and all manner of smaller fish. It was an amazing experience.

From our anchorage surrounded by reefs, I thought it would be a great seamanship feat for the entire crew if we sailed off the anchor the next morning. I gave the crew an explanation of what we were going to do. At least some of them must have understood as it worked fine! The wind was 15 to 20 knots, so, just before the anchor broke away from the seabed, we set the Fore Topsail aback so that it would turn the bow to port. The aft watches were standing by the Fore Mast braces and, when the wind drew close to the beam, we braced the foreyards round. The aft watches then set the Main Topsail and the fore watches set the Fore Course. Chipps, 2nd Engineer, pointed out to me the crystal clear sea-bed beneath us. We felt we could touch every rock and stone. It was very unnerving. I stopped looking over the side, preferring to believe Lesley, Second Mate, when she insisted we were on track and in eight metres of water! We rounded our first beacon and squared the yards whilst we cleared the reefs, before bracing the yards to starboard and altering course to pass down the west side of Cocos Keeling Island. The crew were kept busy; the rope pulling only stopped when we had all the Square Sails set and were bowling along in a SSW'ly direction.

We were potentially faced with days of motoring to get 1000 miles to the south and away from the SE Trade wind which blew steadily at 20 to 25 knots. It was a real treat to have a cracking overnight sail. I was hard on the helmsmen because the better the course they steered, the longer we could sail!! The day was sunny, the night sky clear and the crew happy. The game of murder got underway too. Our course was taking us in the direction of Mauritius, not Australia.

On the 3rd July we started engines and handed sail, but the motion was not pleasant. By the following morning 14 murders had been committed and the Captain had carried out four of them! At 0500 on the 4th the swivel at the head of the main Staysail parted, so a group of us handed the sail. By 0800 the wind had increased to a force 8, and by late morning was regularly hitting 40 knots. We furled the Outer Jib and set the hanked-on Inner Jib. The wind remained a force 8 and we rigged extra safety wires and the 'sailor strainer' netting. Once again I had to ask VC who were wobbly on their feet to remain below decks. Apart from the mid-ships area, the decks were out of bounds due to the angle of heel, up to 40 degrees this time. We continued motoring at half-ahead, with Inner Jib and Mizzen staysail set. Noon: 17° 14'S 093° 43'E Wind: SE 35 to 42 knots

6th July – We knew we had to get further South to be clear of the strong winds. In the morning we were able to set the Fore Topsail, our strongest sail, the wind still hitting 35 or more knots and the seas eight metres high. This sail improved the speed and motion, but we were unable to set more sail because of the real chance that one of the sails would blow out. It became a bit of an endurance test for the crew. Luckily the sun came out which cheered everyone up.

The following day the wind was down to 25 knots, so we set the Main Topsail, both Courses and the Outer Jib and turned the engines off. Under a wonderfully clear night sky we averaged 6 knots. The wind decreased further, enabling us to set the remaining square sails, and we continued sailing "full and by" on a port tack. In the afternoon we handed the Flying Jib and Royals as the wind increased to a force 5. Filming for our video "I Want to Break Free" continued. Oli, the Bosun, filmed and edited whilst Jon, Mate, and Steve, MP, directed. The Voyage crew were now taking noon sights, giving latitudes to within two miles of our true latitude.

Finally the wind and seas calmed down. At 0900 9th July we handed sails, started engines and altered course from 210 to 095 degrees. For the first time we were heading for Australia! The sun came out and the crew were able to laze on deck during the afternoon. As we were almost out of beer and softies, limited numbers of each were being put in the fridge daily.

12th July – In preparation for Department of Environment, Fisheries and Forestry (DAFF) coming onboard in Australia the galley store was deep cleaned. We set Topsails in the morning, but it was only in the afternoon that the wind picked up enough for us to set the rest of the square sails and turn the engines off. We sailed all day with the wind on the port quarter. Heavy rain mid-afternoon gave way to light winds. The heavy rain alternated with downpours and everyone got a thorough soaking. By 2200 we were sailing at 5 knots.

14th July – We sailed all day, despite torrential rain in the afternoon. This did not dampen the enthusiasm everyone had for the Premier of the 'I Want to Break Fremantle' Video filmed by Oli, starring many of the crew. Most crew dressed up for the occasion. Two bottles of cava were opened and everyone had a few sips before the première. The original Freddie Mercury video was shown, followed by our version – to show how close we were to the original, with the extra aspect of being filmed on the ship. It is a truly brilliant video, with most of the PC having a cameo role (watch it on You Tube).

The forecasts had shown the wind picking up from the NW before backing SW and S. This was good for our arrival as it meant great sailing. The biggest wind shift occurred at 0500 on the 15th, so we called out the BMs, and, together with a few crew, braced the yards to port. By 0545 we were on the new tack and the wind increased to 25 knots, remaining so for the rest of the day, giving us a steady speed of 7 knots. In the evening the wind started increasing. By 0500 on 16th we were in a good force 9. We were impressed that our modified Fore T'Gallant was pulling with the best. Our little *Lord Nelson* had morphed into a racing machine. Sleep was impossible and the relief valve on the steering motors kept lifting. We furled the Mizzen Staysail at 0530 but the steering motors were still unhappy. We rigged extra safety lines and the 'sailor strainer nets'. Our speed was about 11 knots and at 0730 we called extra crew on deck to clew up the Main Course. Whilst handing the Course we recorded our highest ever speed of 14.2 knots. I was easing the course sheet; I do not think I have ever eased off a rope with so much weight

on it. Our handiwork, the Fore T'Gallant, was the next to come in. Sadly the few minutes it flogged between handing and getting a gasket on it, were enough to tear the sail. Mid-morning the wind increased so that it was over 52 knots. We did not know the true speed as the gauge only read to 52 knots! In addition the ship heeled to over 46 degrees, off the scale on the inclinometer. These were interesting times, particularly for Dave and Margaret in the galley. The main decks were completely out of bounds; the weather doors shut, storm boards fitted and the crew with mobility issues confined below decks. It was a testing time for the ship, the sails and the crew. We had to make sure that only competent helmsmen steered, which helped with the steering gear. The BMs and Medical Purser were assigned watches. Huge towering swells rose and fell around us, occasionally falling on to the ship. Sleep was not on the agenda. As I rested in my bunk, the groans of the steering gear and the lurching of the ship with huge slaps of water against the side, made sleep impossible. The heavy safe in my cabin made a bid for freedom – the first time I have ever heard of it shifting. Noon to noon we covered 207 nautical miles. In the evening the wind gradually started to decrease. Noon: 32° 17′S 111° 09′E Wind: S'ly 40 knots, gusting 50 knots

17th July – After 0500 the wind dropped below 40 knots for the first time. The seas were still huge. We started engines at 0900 and motor-sailed to keep the speed up. We knew we would miss the 1700 pilot slot which the agent had organised and I was concerned as there was no suitable anchorage. However the pilot called to say he would be available at 2000, a time we were just able to make. We headed towards the bright lights of Fremantle. Had anyone said that morning that we would be alongside that evening, it would have seemed unbelievable. We had a welcoming committee, consisting of a piper, Frazer, StW Project Manager, Kelvin, the agent, Leeuwin crew and various well-wishers. DAFF were to come at 0800 the following day so no shore leave was granted. We had a nice evening in the bar, enjoying the remaining 42 cans of beer the engineers had kept back.

DAFF and Customs spent the following morning onboard. Food items that DAFF took for "deep burial" were salad cream, milk powder, honey, mayonnaise, dried mushrooms, pop-corn and the leather drum from the bar. We did not consider that bad; neither did they. After lunch the VC had free time before we had a last night meal for all in a local Italian. It was good fun and the auction of Charts and flags raised £1000!

After happy hour and my de-brief, volunteers from Leeuwin and Dufken were shown around *Lord Nelson* by our crew. It was Steve, MP's birthday, so we held a surprise party for him.

20th July – Sadly all the VC departed. This had been a brilliant trip, free from the niggles that some of the previous StW trips had. The making of the video "I Want to Break Fremantle" was enormous fun and yielded a great result. Everyone will take away ever-lasting memories.

Our version of the video of
"I Want to Break Fremantle"

Dates		Distances in Nautical Miles				Maximum Wind Force
Start	End	Total	Under Sail	Motor-Sailing	Motoring	
07.06.13	20.07.13	4578	2047	1677	854	10

63

Singapore to Fremantle by Chris Hudson

Wow! What an adventure! I am writing this at 10am in the social area (doubles as a bar) in the company of some very good new friends. As I was on the midnight to 0400 watch, this may take a while to write between naps and cups of tea.

I arrived in Singapore three days early to explore Singapore and help with some basic maintenance on the *Lord Nelson*, a Tall Ship. I found it was a very pleasant way to get to know some of the permanent crew and the layout of Nellie, and begin to get a handle on some of the basic terminology (port-left, starboard-right etc), having never sailed before. Saying that, many voyage crew turned up on the joining day and slotted right in with great support from the captain and her crew. I met my buddy for the trip. He is my watch leader and, although in a wheelchair, he manages a full part in running the ship. I am only his gofer in the very roughest weather when wheelchairs and those who are a little wobbly stay below deck.

It's now day 34 of a 44-day trip from Singapore to Fremantle via Bali and Cocos. We missed Christmas Island due to a heavy swell which closed the bay where we were due to anchor. Sailing the oceans we have to go with the flow and this adds greatly to the experience. Sails up, sails down, sails to port, sails to starboard, engines on, engines off, oh and don't forget the outer jib or was that the main stay sail. Let go the halyard, haul up the sheets. There were some interesting social dynamics within a crew of fifty on a relatively small ship.

Arriving in the Cocos early meant we had extra time on the beautiful tropical Direction Island with a view of Prison Island just along the reef. Great snorkeling, swimming, the simple joy of walking in the surf and lying in the shade of palm trees. Returning to the ship on the inflatable, we were entertained by a school of seven dolphins dancing in our bow wave.

I have had so many wonderful experiences in this trip of a life time. What a buzz! From climbing out on the top sail yard in a force seven (they wouldn't let me up in the force 8 gusting nine, I did ask), being on watch under star-filled skies, seeing a whale and dolphins, and being one of only two people who saw electrostatic firework on the fore T'Gallant yardarm, 'St Elmos Fire' (a once in a blue moon phenomenon).

Having sailed south from the Cocos for eight days, we are now heading due east to my home town of Perth with many great memories of a fantastic trip. Still plenty of sailing to go before I return to work, gardening and caring for my parents. I lived in and around Southampton, England, for 44 years which is where the *Lord Nelson* set sail from last October. It wasn't till I moved to Perth that I found myself sailing on her for part of a round the world trip for people of every possible ability.

Thank you *Lord Nelson* (a mixed ability crew ship) and all who made it possible.

Alan Fisher's Note

You will see in Barbara's report the story of Dan and Anna who got engaged on the voyage. Here is a message I received from Dan in October 2015:

My story from StW 5 is that I proposed to my girlfriend Anna when we crossed the equator going from Singapore to Australia, and she said yes. I actually popped the question during the crossing the line ceremony, so as you can see from the attached pictures, it wasn't the most traditional of marriage proposals!

I was CA on this voyage and I confided in Cookie Dave and Captain Barbara who helped set everything up, so a thank you should go out to them for making it happen.

I hadn't planned to propose prior to the voyage, I just decided to do it shortly after we set sail from Singapore, and we were told we would cross the Equator in a few days. I spent several whole pounds on some red and green string bracelets, took them apart and used them to create a knotted string engagement ring. Once home, we got a jeweller to recreate the string ring out of the more traditional, reassuringly more expensive, precious metals associated with engagement rings.

Anna and Dan. What a setting for a proposal!

A temporary engagement ring.

We got married on 18th April 2014.

Dan Hammond

Dry-docking and Maintenance – Fremantle by Captain Chris Phillips

This was a period of intense activity for all on board for four weeks. The first hurdle was getting the ship properly cleared in to Australia; because we were due to dry-dock, the customs authorities insisted the ship be properly imported. To cut a very long and tedious story short (aspects of which I'm sure I still don't know about), our sponsors Norton Rose Fulbright proved their worth and spent much time and effort negotiating an amicable agreement with the authorities so that the Trust did not have to pay vast sums of money in GST (VAT) for the ship, and so that we could proceed into dry dock as planned. This status took some time to establish; at one point I had the charts out and had started planning a passage straight to New Zealand as it looked as though everything might fall through. However, eventually we were given permission to go into the BAe Systems ship yard a few miles up the coast at Henderson. The yard regulations would not allow us to live on board the ship during the dry dock period, so the whole crew moved off and into accommodation kindly made available to us (at a very good price) at Leeuwin Barracks, a former naval training establishment and now transit accommodation for the Australian Defence Forces. This was a 20-minute car ride from the yard, so every morning a motorcade of hired white Nissans would make its way at the crack of dawn from the barracks to the yard, and back again in the evening.

The dry-docking period was an intensive one, and the works were not helped by poor weather conditions, meaning that the planned blasting and painting was unfinished, leaving large areas of the inside of the bulwarks in grey primer rather than white topcoat. We did carry out a lot of work, however, including some items that were essential for our forthcoming trip to the Antarctic. We were slightly delayed leaving dry dock when some thin steel was discovered in the bows, but I was happy that we discovered it in the yard, not in the ice!

Once we were afloat again, we returned to our berth in Fremantle, next door to the excellent facilities owned by the Leeuwin Ocean Foundation for the upkeep of their barquentine *Leeuwin II*. I must mention the invaluable support we received both from them, in particular their Ops Manager Pete Ripley, and also from the Royal Australian Navy's fleet support unit up the coast at HMAS Stirling, who managed to do a number of engineering jobs for us.

We spent our last week alongside frantically putting the ship back together in time to sail for the next leg to Adelaide.

Lord Nelson reveals her bottom.

Photo: Marcin Dobrowolski

Fremantle Maintenance by Cate Prowse

I arrived in Fremantle and was almost instantly handed a spanner. The dry-dock maintenance, like StW 2 before it, is not remembered fondly by those who've been around long enough to remember voyages where the wind was decent and maintenances that have a relaxed feeling. For me, it was a joy to reconnect with my ship and with people I'd last seen six months before. There were new faces and so much to learn. I took down and sent up sails, painted and chipped; I also learnt how to improvise clothes from bed-sheets after an impromptu trip to the beach, polished my answers to questions on Open Ship and Ship Tours and enjoyed sharing my country with a bunch of grumpy Poms who were distressed to discover Australia has a winter season and that it *will rain*.

High and dry.

Photo: Marcin Dobrowolski

Fremantle Maintenance by Neil Marshall

I joined the army as a seventeen-year old, not sure what I wanted to do but it wasn't sitting in an office. Originally I served as a military policeman, on the beat in Edinburgh and elsewhere in the UK, and then was posted to Germany as a casualty replacement during the first Gulf War. There I worked with Royal Engineers, and after an unwise foray into Military Intelligence, ended up in Bomb Disposal, where I could do lots of more interesting things, like blowing stuff up. I passed the Commando course and worked with Commando

forces around the world, spending time at sea, which I loved, being too stupid to get seasick. We also trained in mountains, desert, jungle and arctic conditions, and I qualified as a RE military diver and military ski instructor.

I was diagnosed with Post-Traumatic Stress Disorder (PTSD), which was exacerbated by my getting a blow to the head with an iron bar. This led to my being admitted to Combat Stress, and then on to retraining

Neil Marshall

Mike Snoxill, one of the voluntary maintainers.

at the Queen Elizabeth College for Disabled People, where I was residential for nine months, and won best student for my carpentry and joinery work.

I was awarded a voyage on *STS Lord Nelson* to commemorate the 200th anniversary of the Battle of Trafalgar, sponsored by the Sir Peter Harrison Foundation. This was the first time I had been back to sea since leaving HM Forces, and I greatly enjoyed the sense of humour. I got involved in carpentry and other maintenance work, and I literally learned the ropes; quite a challenge in view of my head injuries. Also you can't use a spirit level or plumb line on a pitching tall ship. I was recommended as a Bo'sun's Mate, which meant I could do more voluntary work with JST. I don't know of any employers who will take on soldiers with shell shock, which is pretty much an inevitable occupational hazard.

Being at sea gives me peace of mind. You have to focus on the present, deal with unforeseen circumstances and think on your feet. The sea air and good food certainly helps! I did more and more voyages, progressing from day and week voyages in UK waters to European waters, then my first transatlantic crossing to the Caribbean. Soon we started hearing rumours of a global circumnavigation, which turned into Sail the World.

I believe I was involved in about 40% of StW, from the manic month of pre-departure maintenance, to the home-coming parties in London and Southampton two years later. It was an exhausting project, from the retrospective fitting of air-conditioning, still working on it as the ship crossed the equator for the first time en route to Rio de Janeiro; working with Australian Health and Safety officials in the dry dock at Fremantle; cutting out the forward heads (toilets) to access the hull; rebuilding the heads en route to Adelaide; the Southern Ocean and Cape Horn voyage, which was an exercise in working with injuries sustained, to the final leg from Halifax to London.

I was extremely privileged to be involved in the Sail the World project, and proud that we got the ship around the globe.

Photo: Marcin Dobrowolski

Voyage 16 – Fremantle to Adelaide by Captain Chris Phillips

This voyage was the start of our close involvement with the Dutch tall ships, *Europa*, *Tecla* and *Oosterschelde*, who were due to join us for the Australian maritime festivals and the Fleet Review in Sydney. They had already joined us briefly in Fremantle as they arrived in Australia, and the first festival would be in Adelaide. We left Fremantle a day late, still in a certain amount of disarray after the dry-docking and refit period, but soon Nellie was vaguely shipshape again, and we headed down the coast of Western Australia and had a motor-sailing passage round to the port of Albany on the SW corner of the continent; thus we rounded the second of the three Great Capes, Cape Leeuwin.

We spent only one night alongside in Albany, most of the crew being entertained in one of the local hostelries by BM Neil Marshall's uncle and aunt, who lived nearby. There was a certain amount of local press interest, as visits by international tall ships are evidently rare in the port! The reason for our short stay was simply that we still had the whole Great Australian Bight to cross

in order to get to Adelaide, and our deadline for arrival was strict, given our planned attendance at the festival there.

The passage was seven days, mostly spent under sail, just using engines when the wind dropped or at the end of the passage to make our ETA when the wind turned against us. Unfortunately, time did not allow us to visit the Spencer Gulf or Port Lincoln, the ports where the last windjammers loaded their grain cargoes in the 1920s and 30s.

We arrived on time for our pilot at Port Adelaide, and then had the fun experience of forming a not-so-orderly queue for the lifting bridge, which had inconveniently decided not to lift for us, *Europa*, *Tecla*, *Oosterschelde* and probably a host of other vessels! After a tricky berthing manoeuvre in breezy conditions, we finally made it alongside and were mobbed by the full force of the South Australian media.

Fremantle to Adelaide by Cate Prowse

When the ship left Fremantle, I went with it, on my first Watch Leader trip. My watch were fantastic, as much a delight to talk to in the depths of the Middle Watch (0000-0400) as they were at high noon. In Adelaide, my parents were there to meet us, with half a ship's worth of spares and the Barbie warming up. One morning meeting, I'd been asked to tell them to put the barbeque on and I, still adjusting to British sarcasm, had obliged. What should have been a 20 person gathering for permanent crew became a 40 person party to remember. Several people from the ship have suggested my parents would never invite any of them back; on the contrary, my mother was pleased to host a group of people who, midway through the evening, trooped inside to enthusiastically do the washing up. (Though my father was a little surprised to find a blind girl drying the glasses, and my mother discovered a usually wheelchair bound guy taking a pig-back tour of the upstairs.)

Fremantle to Adelaide by Jarryd van den Heuvel

My time upon the *Lord Nelson* was an experience that I will not forget quickly. It was one of the few times I have felt that we were all treated equally in a large group situation. We all had the same opportunities and responsibilities to do everything to the best of our ability.

We were set into watches with a Watch Leader to help us orientate ourselves on the ship. This was especially helpful for people like me who have had no previous experience on a tall ship, and our Watch Leader taught us the order of the ship and looked out for us.

View from aloft.

Photo: Russ

When it came to setting the sails or furling them, everyone got involved, either going aloft or pulling on the ropes; no one was excluded. As time went on and people started to learn their way around the ship, the permanent crew gave us more and more jobs, e.g. go and slack the bunt lines or clew lines.

The rosters were varied each day on a 10-day cycle, so we were rotated across the whole range of chores on the ship. This meant that everyone had the opportunity to do every watch period on the ship from 00:00 to 00:00 and to help out in the galley, as well as swab the decks.

When my Watch Leader, Cate, had mess duty she put me in charge of our watch for 24 hours. During this time I had two watches, afternoon and night as well as the morning meeting to go to. This meeting is where the permanent crew discuss progress and any issues that have arisen. My time as Watch Leader was interesting and a big learning curve; I had to make sure that the eight people in my crew were paying attention to the horizon if they were on look out, that the person on the helm was steering the correct course and that the log was done every hour. The safety of the whole crew depended on it; I wouldn't want the ship to founder on MY watch.

We all had an opportunity to go aloft no matter our disability; I saw people in wheel chairs pull themselves up to the platform or get hoisted up.

The First Mate lost his voice towards the end of the voyage so he got me to yell 2-6 Heave (command for pulling ropes). It was an interesting assignment for me as I have difficulty projecting my voice, so this was a great training exercise.

While we were sailing from Fremantle to Albany the weather was rough, with a head wind all the way. Must admit I felt very queasy but at least I wasn't the only one. Loved Albany, the town was pretty and the people were very friendly....especially at the pub!

View from bowsprit.

Photo: Russ

Sailing the Bight was amazing, with eight days of nothing but ocean. I was stunned on day 4 to find a dragonfly floating around; I wondered where it had come from. There were lots of dolphins and a few whales as well as albatross and what I think were shearwaters. I was lucky enough to see "the green flash" at sunset, but sadly not the southern lights (Aurora Australis) I was hoping for. A few times I saw dolphins surfing on our bow wave; they were having a lot of fun.

... more dolphins.

The midnight to 4 a.m. watch was VERY cold! During the night watch it was comforting to see the lights of the three Dutch ships on the horizon; the *Oosterschelde*, *Barque Europa* and *Tecla* had gone ahead of us.

Coming into Adelaide ahead of schedule, we had to go around and around in circles to waste time while we were waiting for the pilot to come and escort us into harbour. Needless to say our log for those few hours must look very funny with just a circle with arrows on it.

We stayed in Pt Adelaide for 3 ½ days, in which time I explored the township on my own or with other crew. It was a nice little town. While there we were all invited to a Navy party that I enjoyed, especially the historical aspect. It was fun to talk to the visitors on Open Day.

Dates		Distances in Nautical Miles				Maximum Wind Force
Start	End	Total	Under Sail	Motor-Sailing	Motoring	
17.08.13	31.08.13	1431	413	742	276	7

Photo: Simone Neumuller

Voyage 17 – Adelaide to Melbourne by Captain Barbara Campbell

From Adelaide we motored in calm conditions towards Kangaroo Island, taking advantage of the flat seas to carry out assisted climbs. Two of our voyage crew in wheelchairs hoisted themselves aloft using the self-ascending gear, whilst other crew had the security of a rope as they climbed aloft. It was a great day to be on deck and everyone enjoyed the afternoon. The wind started to fill in at 2200 as we entered Backstairs Passage.

By morning we had a sailing breeze from the Northeast and after breakfast, all hands were called on deck to set sail. We set all square sails plus the fore and aft sail, including the Spanker. From sedate sailing at 4 knots during the morning, the wind picked up, necessitating the handing of Royals, T'Gallants and Spanker; we were still making 7 knots at midnight.

On 4th September we continued sailing eastwards under reduced canvas, making 5 or 6 knots in dull overcast conditions. During the night we squared the fore and main yards as the wind drew aft. With many eager hands we sent down the Fore Topsail and sent back up the Topsail with the JST logo on it. We hoped to sail overnight but at 2200 the wind faded away so we clewed up sail and motored on one engine overnight, the speed required being only 2.5 knots!

Approaching Melbourne.

The pilot boarded at 0900 on the 6th, and under Topsails we entered the notorious 'Rip' at Port Phillip Heads. *Lord Nelson* looked impressive, with the ship apparently sailing through surf. The moment was captured by a photographer on the beach at Point Lonsdale. On passage towards Williamstown, we had happy hour and sail stowing. The Fore Topsail with the JST logo was kept set for Jacquetta and Harry Cator* to admire, as they came out by launch to greet the ship. Shortly afterwards we anchored in Hobson's Bay, close to Williamstown; this was where the early Tall Ships had anchored as Williamstown was the original port of Melbourne. In the evening we had a BBQ – not exactly BBQ weather but we were all wrapped up and it was a successful evening.

Cooks or pyromaniacs? Marco and Marcin.

Photo: Rob McDonald

The following morning we weighed anchor and moored alongside our berth at the historic Workshops Pier by the 'Seaworks Museum'. Three Dutch Tall ships; *Oosterschelde*, *Europa* and *Tecla* followed us in. There were crowds of visitors on the quay so we had an impromptu open ship from 1300 to 1500. Most crew went ashore for a meal and ended up in the 'Pirates Tavern' at 'Seaworks', dancing to live music.

The 8th was a bright sunny day. Following a final Happy Hour, Captain's debrief and an early lunch, the VC departed. They had enjoyed a cracking voyage, almost 60% under sail. Nearly all the crew were Australian. They all had a great time and we certainly drew the crowds and wowed the media.

* **Jacquetta Cator** has been the Jubilee Sailing Trust's President since 2007. It was she who thought up the name *Tenacious* and officially named the ship at a ceremony presided over by Prince Andrew on 6 April 2000. Jacquetta first became involved in the JST in the early 1980s after encouraging her husband, Francis Cator, to take on the role of Chairman of the Trustees. Francis, as Vice-Chairman of the merchant bankers Schroder Wagg & Co, was a highly respected figure in the City as well as an experienced sailor. Brought up by a mother who overcame serious disability caused by polio in childhood, he had both an understanding of the needs of disabled people and a positive desire to be of practical help. He was a very key figure in raising the funds required to establish the JST as a major charity and build its first ship, *Lord Nelson*. Francis made the JST his life's work after he retired from the City, and when he died in 2007, his wife Jacquetta remained deeply involved in order to keep his memory alive in the Trust's daily life. Jacquetta herself brings her own understanding of disability, having worked tirelessly for Riding for the Disabled as well as the JST. The contribution of Francis and Jacquetta to the JST cannot be over-estimated and their inspiration was always to enable disabled people to overcome their disabilities and take part in normal life, as Francis' mother had done.

One of her sons, **Harry Cator**, lives in Australia. Until *Lord Nelson* visited Australia, he had never seen the ship in which his parents were so involved. Following the success of the visit, JST Australia has been established, and Harry has recently become Chairman of JST Australia.

Mark, bell polishing.

Adelaide to Melbourne by Jarryd den Heuvel

We picked up new crew in Adelaide, which began the whole process of having to learn new names and teach them the run of the ship. We also had a new Captain come on board.

Coming out of Adelaide we were joined by the *One And All*, and we gave each other "three cheers" for a safe journey. From here we had great winds, allowing us to sail most of the way; we hardly used the motor, and still arrived in Melbourne in just six days, so we had to moor overnight in the Bay. There was a beautiful sunset over Melbourne town and by morning we were surrounded by four other tall ships which had joined us overnight in the Bay.

We began the day bright and early to have brekkie before the pilot arrived to escort us into harbour. I was on starboard lookout, an experience I enjoyed even though I had no idea what I was meant to be looking out for. When we finally docked I was amazed to see a black swan swimming around our hull.

We had a few hours to explore Williamstown before the arrival of the public to come and see our tall ships. Lunch was pizza and beer on Williamstown Main Street. Nice! Hint...Pirate Bar on the docks serves Baileys and Hot Chocolate...

Mum arrived the next day to collect me and to bring my grandfather's ashes, as the Captain had offered to sprinkle him at sea as they sailed out of the heads of Pt Phillip Bay, the same way he had come into Australia 59 years ago.

It was a sad day for me to have to leave the ship and all my new friends, of which I have made many. Some of the people I met were incredibly inspiring; I hope to keep this experience with me forever as a reminder of what can be achieved with a little inspiration and effort.

Thank you JST, *Lord Nelson* and the crew and STI Host Bursary Scheme for making this incredible experience possible for me.

Surfing the 'Rip' at Port Philip Heads, Melbourne.

Photo: Chris Bridge

Adelaide to Melbourne by Cate Prowse

On to Melbourne, and it really became clear that with every Aussie port we visited the party was just going to grow and grow. Already in Fremantle, two Aussie and four European tall ships was more than I'd even seen before. In Melbourne it was more again and the party was bigger; more stalls, more bunting, free drinks in pubs for those sailing on the ships. That atmosphere was just a taste of what Australia had in store and I'm so glad I got the opportunity to celebrate tall ships in my home country.

Wheelchair user hauling herself aloft using our new 'self ascend' gear.

	Dates		Distances in Nautical Miles				Maximum Wind Force
	Start	End	Total	Under Sail	Motor-Sailing	Motoring	
	01.09.13	08.09.13	540	299	79	162	6

Voyage 18 – Melbourne to Hobart by Captain Barbara Campbell

On the afternoon of joining day we packed in as much training as we could, as there was a fireworks display from a nearby barge that evening. Various friends came on board to watch the display from the bridge of *Lord Nelson*, creating a great atmosphere.

The pilot boarded at 0800 the following morning and all the tall ships milled around whilst waiting for the Parade of Sail to start. We set Topsails and followed our designated route; the crew had time to practise bracing too. After lunch the wind fell light and we clewed up the Topsails and motored south to an anchorage off Rye Pier late afternoon. The crew had a BBQ on board whilst I had a working dinner ashore at the Blairgowrie Yacht Club, talking about *Lord Nelson* and the JST.

We commenced weighing anchor at 0815 on the 15th and were soon proceeding, with the other tall ships (*Europa*, *Oosterschelde*, *Young Endeavour*, *Windward Bound*), towards the 'Rip' at Port Phillip Heads. Slack water was at 1000 and we were to be there at 1030.

Parade of Sail.

Photo: Dave Shine

We set fore and aft sail, Topsails, Main T'Gallant and Fore Course and the crew were kept on their toes as we initially squared then braced the yards. We set all sail and the crew did not have a breather from rope pulling until the pilot departed at 1116. The Captain of *Soren Larsen* called us to say that we looked great with everything set. There had been much discussion about whether to go east or west round Tasmania. The East is generally the preferred route but, to my mind there was only one way to go. The forecast was for 40 knot east winds for the next two days and eventually the other Captains agreed it best to go down the west side. At 1700, the wind, which had slowly been picking up all day, reached 15 knots and we handed the Royals and Fore T'Gallant. The seas started to build and few ate dinner. By midnight the wind was Easterly 20 to 25 knots and we furled the Main T'Gallant. Unfortunately sleep was not easy in the foc's'le as the anchor could not be fully tightened due to a change in the arrangement in dry dock, and the banging kept the crew awake.

The crew really were a poorly lot by morning when we were making 7 to 8 knots in 35 to 45 knot winds. The seas and swell were rough with the wind on the beam. We rolled to 30 degrees a few times. By mid-morning the crew were in one of two camps – they either thought it brilliant sailing or they wanted to get off the ship. At least we did not have the medical problem that *Windward Bound* suffered when a watertight door to the deck slammed and broke three fingers of the Captain's hand. At noon we rounded the NW point of Tasmania with gusts of wind reaching 50 knots. I told everyone it would soon go down and by 1600 the wind was 20 knots and decreasing. With the seas calmer most crew managed some dinner. Despite being in the lee of Tasmania, we sailed slowly overnight in 10 knots of wind.

By 0900 on the 17th the wind was ENE and we were 35 miles to the west of Port Davey. We clewed up sail and had a swift motor to a sheltered anchorage in the North Arm of Port Davey. During the day, the other tall ships anchored near us in one of the many inlets. Strictly speaking it was a pilotage area but collectively, we Captains considered it a 'Port Of Refuge' from the 30 knot East winds round the southern Capes of Tasmania. We were amazed by the huge numbers of dolphins as we approached the anchorage. Port Davey is a National Park and the only access is by boat or a

Departing Melbourne under sail.

Photo: Dave Shine

five day hike. It reminded me of NW Scotland. The crew loved the anchorage and we had a short quiz in the evening. With eight guys and girls from the Australian Army now recovered from seasickness, it was a fun evening.

I had planned on sailing at lunchtime on the 18th but the forecast showed the strong east winds to the south easing and becoming south-west, so I delayed sailing. In the morning we carried out assisted climbs followed by quiet time. We weighed anchor at 1600 and motored to the south. Gaskets were loosed and we were all ready to set sail with a very keen crew, but the wind remained Easterly. In the evening heavy drizzle hung round us.

All night I had been waiting to set sail but the forecast wind shift did not happen. The overnight drizzle turned to persistent rain. We set sail at 0930 and sailed until 1200. As we approached our anchorage at Adventure Bay, we heard that our pilot time had been brought forward to 0930/20th, which would necessitate a 0500 start. I called up and asked if we could anchor in the north end of D'Entrecasteaux Channel, despite it being a pilotage area. Sense prevailed and the pilots permitted our entry. Three hours later we entered this beautiful stretch of water and were soon at anchor in the aptly named 'Snug Bay'. We liked 'Snug Bay' though it meant the Voyage crew could not go ashore at Adventure Bay. In the evening we had a Horse Race which was brilliant fun and raised over 500 dollars.

We weighed anchor the following morning and it was an amazing sight as all the tall ships proceeded to the pilot station. *Europa* outdid us all as she set most of her sails. *Lady Nelson*, a small replica brig, looked absolutely splendid too. The wind increased to 15 knots from astern and we were a grand spectacle. We picked the pilot up at the later time of 1300 and were berthed by 1430. The crowds were already on the quayside – such is the eager anticipation from the Hobartians. We sent down one sail for repair and set the mesh Topsail.

After Happy Hour on 21st we were Open Ship from 1000 to 1200 and from 1400 to 1800. Apparently 5,000 people visited the port between the hours of 1000 and 1800! We fielded two teams in a fun 'Maritime Games', with one of our teams coming second in the tug of war. A crew member in a wheelchair was part of the team in the obstacle course and all the crowd were behind the *Lord Nelson* teams.

On the 22nd we had the Captain's debrief, a quick happy hour and smunch, which included a birthday cake for Watch Leader Heather, 82 years young that day.

One of our teams doing well in the Tug of War, Hobart.
Photo: Ellen Shine

This was a good voyage with lots of positive feedback. The eight Australian military personnel were not used to the delay between being asked to do something and the doing of it, as it took time to get the VC into place. They also found it slightly frustrating when we said we would set sail and then the wind did not play ball and we had to wait several hours. However they enjoyed knowing the plan in advance – something they apparently were not used to! At the end of the day it was a great trip, despite the bumpy weather at the start. We sailed for 57% of the total distance, which included the long motor across Port Philip bay and the motor round the south of Tasmania.

Photo: Craig Millsom

Melbourne to Hobart by Rudi Bianchi

When I first became aware of such a voyage, I must admit my nautical urges increased. I had spent most of my life at sea, firstly in the Royal Australian Navy and then the Merchant Navy, so it is fair to say that the salt content in my veins was considerably high. I spoke with my wife, who thought it was a good idea but, like myself, wondered if at 75 years of age I would be accepted. My friend Terry Moran also expressed interest and with much trepidation we applied, fully aware that a return email with "Thanks but no thanks" might arrive. We had both maintained a good level of fitness and hoped that would help. To our delight we were accepted, and so "Melbourne here we come" became our war cry.

The moment arrived and we embarked on to the *Lord Nelson*. I knew space would be at a premium, but the lockers made even the old Navy lockers look luxurious. One wag suggested we may have to fold our tooth brushes. Bunks were adequate but I can't imagine a basketballer thinking the same. We were placed in the forecastle section of 18 bunks. The wash basin, toilet and shower were contained in the one unit and two of these serviced the forecastle crew. With fresh water at a premium the wet, lather, wash and then wash off routine was the order of the day. We realised very quickly "It ain't the Hilton". There were a few tall ships berthed, the biggest of which was the "Europa", which was quite majestic. On the first day we were split into four watches with an assigned watch leader. We would keep watches, taking turns at the helm, on lookout and maintaining the ship's log. We all donned harnesses and climbed up the masts and out on to the yard arms. Thrill level very high, comfort level not so high. With lots of entertainment on the wharf, not to mention thousands of sightseers, a relaxing beer in the bar rounded the first night off. A huge fireworks display that night and it all seemed so civil and relaxing.

The next day we motored down Port Philip bay and anchored off Sorrento. The bay was crammed with craft of all shapes and sizes and when a huge

Everyone gets to steer.

Photo: Craig Millsom

container ship "thump, thump, thumped" past us, it was impossible not to notice how small we were. The Skipper (a wonderful lady, Barbara Campbell) attended a reception ashore and we lazed back, unaware of what was to come. The next day we up anchored and headed out through the Rip into Bass Strait. The odds on the strait being warm and calm are approximately the same as winning the lottery and it did not disappoint. After some intership consultation it was decided to head down between King Island and mainland Tasmania and proceed down the west coast. It was at this point that the voyage completely changed its personality. We corkscrewed, which involved both motions (pitching and rolling) and the vomit bags were well patronised. Being biodegradable, they could be thrown over the side, and we were constantly reminded to use the lee side for obvious reasons. With constant pitching and rolling, tiredness became a factor and, even though bunk boards had to be placed to avoid falling out, sleeping was not a problem. The port anchor could not be drawn snugly into its hawspipe and as it sat proud, the anchor flukes would hit the ship's hull with a resounding bang as we drove into the oncoming sea. Working the helm on watch was a real test, as the ship's head wandered all over the place. The big winner was speed and we made good progress down the west coast. As the winds came from the deep south they carried a chill that was cutting. The midnight to 0400 watch was particularly prone to these cold winds. The top sails on the fore and main masts (which, if I recollect, were called the Fore Royal and the Main Royal) were stowed as they tended to push us over, with no value in speed attained. Throughout all of this, Davy the Cook (surely the most important man on ANY ship?) kept us fed, though I am quite sure the intakes dropped.

Strahan was given a miss and, escorted by magical dolphins, we anchored in Port Davey and collectively got our breath back. Quiz contests and horse racing in the bar at night went a long way to explaining why a ship is the ultimate breeding ground for that wonderful word "camaraderie". Whenever asked what I miss most away from the sea that magic word pops up.

At this point I must dedicate part of my report to some special people we had on board. The *Lord Nelson* has the capability of carrying people with disabilities and, amongst our crew, there were some in wheelchairs, with cerebral palsy and other handicaps. This included a Scottish paratrooper who lost a leg virtue of an I.E.D. in Afghanistan. One cerebral palsy sufferer had medals as a swimmer in the Paralympic games. The drive and attitude shown by these people, considering the terrible hand given to them by fate, was inspirational and flowed throughout the ship. Our watch had a young man who was wheelchair bound yet attended every watch, and was undoubtedly the best helmsman. Their collective stoicism was a tonic to us all.

After Port Davey we headed south into even colder winds, and finally rounded the southernmost tip of Tasmania. Even though the winds had abated, a constant swell reminded us all that King Neptune was still the boss. We anchored in Snug Bay and waited in a group prior to entering the Derwent River and Hobart.

As expected, we were greeted by many small craft and the crowds were huge, considering Hobart has just 200,000 people. A run ashore was on everyone's mind, and my first duty was to relieve a sea food restaurant of its stock of scallops (crumbed of course).

Our voyage had ended. I can still see lithe Bosun's Mate, Alice' scampering up the masts like a well drilled acrobat. Big Jon's (the Mate) booming voice coming over like a calming tonic. Reminiscing with the skipper of the old days in the Merchant Navy (Royal Docks, Liverpool, Glasgow and Southampton). Moments to treasure. As we left "Nellie" I found it hard to comprehend how small it was (my last ship in the Merchant Navy was a 220,000 ton tanker), yet its character was just as big. In conclusion it was cold, wet, windy, rough, uncomfortable, tough and I absolutely loved it!

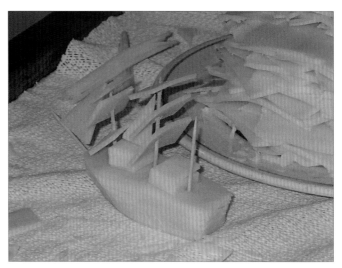

Photo: Dave Shine

	Dates		Distances in Nautical Miles				Maximum Wind Force
	Start	End	Total	Under Sail	Motor-Sailing	Motoring	
	13.09.13	22.09.13	538	304	56	178	7

Photo: Dave Shine

Voyage 19 – Hobart to Sydney by Captain Barbara Campbell

24th September – The crew joined in Hobart and training finished with rope practice after dinner.

The following morning we had a prompt start with the pilot joining soon after 0900 for the Parade of Sail out of Hobart. The wind was 25 knots and very gusty but all eight of the tall ships managed to form a line. We looked magnificent as we sailed in a good following breeze. Many local boats followed us down Derwent Water, only turning back because of impending nightfall. The bad weather forecast had given me a sleepless night and though I had pushed to get my Pilot's Exemption Certificate for Port Arthur and Wineglass Bay, I decided to sail past Port Arthur as we still had a good sailing wind. We rounded Tasman Island at 1900 but the wind soon started to head us so we handed sail. Then followed a bumpy night northwards in a light Northerly wind.

By dawn we were approaching Wineglass Bay, which is normally reached by a walk of several hours. Most of the crew were mighty grateful when we were tucked up in Wineglass Bay as strong Westerly winds blew all day. Some looked longingly at the remote crescent-shaped beach but persistent heavy rain was not encouraging, and we did not run the crew ashore. In the evening we had a fun quiz.

We sailed off the anchor at 1000 on 27th without using engines, but the wind was very fickle, so we motored north from midday. From 1600 the light northerly winds quickly increased to NNW force 6, resulting in another uncomfortable motor all night. The crew had not got the hang of the ship's motion, and fish pie, banoffee pie and soft drinks were liberally spilled in the lower mess.

The forecasts showed 28th as the best day for crossing the Bass Strait, as we would have a sailing wind. We were level with the north of Tasmania at 0700 and at 0845 called all hands on deck as the wind had freed enough to enable us to set sail. We were soon making

7 to 8 knots under Topsails, Courses and Outer Jib. Initially the motion was fine; however the forecast was for 30 to 40 knot winds, not the 50 knot winds we started experiencing! After 1800 we started having gusts of 50 knots, occasionally more, though we had no way of measuring wind speeds over 50 knots. In between gusts the wind averaged 35 knots. The night was very dark and the decks were out of bounds with the weather doors shut. One of the other Tall Ships near us recorded 65 knots of wind. From 1900 to 2000 we covered 11 nautical miles. We kept the wind just abaft the beam in the gusts. At 2015, in a gust of over 50 knots the aged Main Course sail succumbed. I had thought about handing it but felt the decks were too dangerous. After it tore we ran before the winds and clewed up what we could of it. Half an hour later the Outer Jib ripped; at least it was repairable. The wind was a force 9 or 10 for 10 hours. Whilst this was going on, the Engineers had their own problems, with the low level alarm on the hydraulic tank for the steering pumps going off each time we heeled. Tamsin, 2nd Engineer, topped up the tank in 50 knots of wind, without spilling any oil; the tank is on the chartroom roof! It was a long night as we lurched our way across the Bass Strait. We later heard that the Dutch Schooner, *Oosterschelde*, broke 2 booms, and that the *Barque Europa* lost the top 4.5 metres of her Mizzen mast. Our VC coped really well throughout.

Dawn welcomed us with decreasing seas and 25 knot west winds. Everyone felt exhilarated, though tired. By 0800 the wind was a mere 12 knots and everyone tucked into a huge breakfast. Kevin King, our liaison officer for Sydney, had negotiated a free berth and free pilot in the port of Eden. Eden is just inside the State of NSW and is the only proper port on this section of coast. An old Whaling Station, Eden is accustomed to lots of yachts limping in after bad weather during the Sydney to Hobart race. A small town of 3,500 welcomed us and many visited the ship. There was one pub, two restaurants, a fisherman's club and lots of great fish and chip shops. Eden catered for all and the crew liked the place and the friendly locals. There was a stunning beach a mile away and a great Whaling Museum. We heard tales of woe from *Lady Nelson* who had motored across almost underwater. The MCA would certainly not allow her out of sheltered waters! In the calm of Port eden we sent down the damaged Main Course and Outer Jib.

After taking the voyage photo on 30th we had assisted climbs. The pilot came for a look around with his children and told us we could stay another night. This news was warmly welcomed by VC and PC alike.

1st October – Jon, the Mate, took the ship off the berth; outside the port we had photos taken with the brig *Lady Nelson*. We caught up with *Soren Larsen* and had a frustrating time trying to sail up the coast. At

Big Sea!
Photo: Robin McConcille

least the sun shone. Whales and dolphins abound on this coast and we had plenty of sightings.

The following morning we entered Jervis Bay, 90 miles south of Sydney. This large, sheltered bay was where 15 warships were at anchor in readiness for the Fleet Review in Sydney. We slowly motored past the warships, a police launch informing us we could go no closer. Due to the 25 knot northerly winds, we decided to anchor until 1530. The crew remembered most of what they had to do for sailing off the anchor, so we had another go and managed to sail across Jervis Bay and a short distance up the coast. At 1915 we handed sail and motored into head winds.

RIP. Our 21 year old main course – the Bass Strait.

As forecast, the wind became westerly overnight and we set Topsails at 0400 on the 3rd. This gave us 4 to 5 knots in 25 knots of wind. We were due to have a photo shoot with *Young Endeavour*, and Max Mudie (BM, professional photographer and son of the *Lord Nelson's* designer Colin Mudie) took some splendid photos of us. We kept our sails set all the way to Sydney Heads in the hope that *Young Endeavour* would join us. In the end, still under sail, we put our engines slow astern and still struggled to go slowly enough. Just after passing the North Head we handed sail as the course into the harbour was straight into wind. The ships at the front went too slowly and

we had a huge bottleneck at the back of the line. In the end we anchored for an hour as it was taking a long time to berth the ships ahead, given the confined space and the strong winds. Our berth outside the Australian National Maritime Museum was particularly tight but we got alongside mid-afternoon. As soon as the gangway was rigged the press descended. A number of interviews later, including four for radio, I joined the other Captains for an evening reception. Most of our crew headed to the oldest pub in Sydney, the "Lord Nelson". Not surprisingly they got a big welcome! The management even invited the Permanent Crew for dinner the night of the 7th.

After a last Happy Hour, Captain's de-brief and smoko, a very happy crew left the ship.

Despite the rough seas everyone loved the voyage and all the comments were amazingly positive. The Voyage Crew praised the skills of the PC, especially during the crossing of the Bass Strait.

After the voyage crew departed we readied ourself for the fleet review, where we had a designated anchorage in Sydney Harbour.

Licking our wounds, Port Eden.

Dates		Distances in Nautical Miles				Maximum Wind Force
Start	End	Total	Under Sail	Motor-Sailing	Motoring	
24.09.13	04.10.13	696	301	257	138	10

Bass Strait Crossing by Tom Sag

On Saturday morning (September 28th) we passed the north east corner of Tasmania and entered the Bass Strait. By this time the wind had changed to WNW which meant we could sail, as we were heading NNE for Gabo Island near the Victoria NSW border. After breakfast it was all hands on deck to set the Fore and Main Topsails and Courses and the Outer Jib. However we had to hand the Mizzen Staysail to avoid interference with the Main Course. With all these sails up our speed increased to 6-7 knots as the wind strengthened to 25-35 knots and later to 30-45 knots and more! We achieved speeds of 8-9 knots and later still we got up to 10.7 knots on our 1230-1600 watch. Steering became easier as the speed increased but keeping one's balance became more difficult as the ship developed a lean of about 30 degrees to starboard. There were plenty of rails etc to hang on to on the bridge and in the chart room but things were more difficult down below. Apparently the next watch achieved a speed of 11.7 knots!

After dinner Captain Barbara called for volunteers to hand the Mizzen Staysail. This involved hauling on lines on the low starboard side of the ship, and I got drenched by the 3-4 metre waves coming over the side as I foolishly was not wearing wet weather gear on my lower half. I decided not to volunteer to help hand the Main Course which had developed a large rip, to avoid another drenching before our 0000 to 0400 watch. While I was drying out below in the bar lounge I got thrown out of my chair and ended up landing in little Heather's lap. Poor old Dave Bond did not fare so well. He lost his balance up on deck after a stint on the wheel, and came down the stairs with injuries to his face and arms and a big bleeding gash on his leg which required many stitches. However Liz, the medical purser (a doctor) and Alison (nurse) from our watch patched him up quite nicely and he slowly recovered during the next few days.

For our midnight watch the conditions were just as severe as before and much colder. We were ordered to stay on the high port side of the ship, and where possible clip on and stay inside the bridge enclosure which was now equipped with perspex screens to keep the wind out. During our watch we achieved speeds of 10-11 knots for a while but this dropped to 7-9 knots towards the end of the watch, when the wind strength decreased to a "modest" 25-30 knots as we neared the end of Bass Strait. We reached the NSW coast by about 0600. After breakfast we made good progress towards Eden in nice blue water and saw several whales and dolphins.

Easy steering with one hand in all this wind.

Voyage 20 – Sydney to Auckland – Tall Ships Race by Captain Chris Phillips

I joined the ship again in Sydney after a few weeks' break in the UK, and immediately set to making sure everything was as ready as possible for the race to New Zealand. A few sails had been sent down for repair after the excitements of the Bass Strait in the previous voyage, during which several of the fleet had sustained damage. We had to ensure that the sails were all bent on again before departure, as well as enjoying the hospitality that had been laid on for us, and, of course, also the Fleet Review. I was still suffering jetlag, so Barbara, who had not yet left, did most of the hard work!

When it came to departure, it was a blustery day, and I had a rather uncooperative pilot who made the departure fairly fraught and more difficult than it should have been, even from our rather awkward berth.

We got clear eventually, and joined the fleet awaiting the start of the race between the Heads. The gun sounded, and we crossed the line first (well, after *Spirit*

Sailing past the Opera House.

of New Zealand, who, in her enthusiasm, crossed before the gun!), setting sail and getting out to sea and clear of the rest of the fleet.

The weather for the first few days of the race produced some exciting sailing conditions, as well as some

91

challenging wind shifts, and we made good progress across the Tasman Sea, though unfortunately falling into a position near the rear of the fleet. However, the crew were enjoying the sailing, which was the important thing.

The last couple of days of the race, as we approached Cape Reinga and then the finish line, promised to be challenging in a different way, with the wind dropping to light airs. In Nellie's case though, the race was cut short by the failure of our main royal backstay fitting at the masthead, and we suddenly found that the main mast was not as well supported as it should have been. This persuaded me that we ought to get into port as soon as possible, in order to arrange a repair of the fitting. I retired Nellie from the race and left all the other ships wallowing in the calms, whilst we went on ahead to the Bay of Islands to clear in. As it happened, we were not very much ahead of most of the ships, as some were far enough ahead to finish the race. As we lay at anchor waiting to clear in off the town of Russell, we offloaded the offending fitting to go to a shipyard in Whangarei to be re-engineered. We then went in alongside to be cleared in before the local community could welcome us with a traditional Maori Powhiri ceremony.

For the next leg of the trip we joined *Spirit of New Zealand* and *Young Endeavour* to visit Great Barrier Island, and put some of the VC ashore there for a leg-stretch, before we headed on down independently to Whangarei to retrieve and fit our repaired backstay fittings (we took the opportunity to reinforce the foremast fitting as well), and have a couple of other jobs done in preparation for Antarctica whilst we were there. We spent the day in the shipyard, whilst the voyage crew explored the town, and then in the evening we set off again, down towards Auckland and the welcoming committee there.

The voyage ended with a parade of sail into the harbour, and the usual Tall Ships Race festivities.

Parade of sail into Auckland Harbour.

Racing close to *Europa*.

Dates		Distances in Nautical Miles				Maximum Wind Force
Start	End	Total	Under Sail	Motor-Sailing	Motoring	
08.10.13	27.10.12	1514	954	317	243	9

Rob McDonald
Photo: Marcin Dobrowolski

Voyage 21 – Auckland to Wellington by Captain Chris Phillips

This was the first of our short voyages around New Zealand, and we were joined by a multinational crew for our departure from Auckland in another parade of sail. Once clear of Auckland harbour, we parted company with the rest of the fleet and headed east towards East Cape, passing White Island, an active volcano, on the way. The passage was mostly under sail, but we were by now learning the vagaries of antipodean weather, and in particular how quickly the wind can shift! We made a very successful port stop in Napier, where we were given free berthing and pilotage. After the hectic timetable of the tall ships festivals and race, it was nice to be operating independently once again, and the stop-off was very relaxed.

After Napier we were joined once again by *Young Endeavour*, and we both made our way into the beautiful scenery of the Marlborough Sounds, where we anchored for a night. We then had an exhilarating sail across the Cook Strait, and had to force our way into Wellington Harbour against a stiff breeze. However, we made it alongside, and the VC had a last night ashore in the capital of New Zealand.

Dates		Distances in Nautical Miles				Maximum Wind Force
Start	End	Total	Under Sail	Motor-Sailing	Motoring	
27.10.13	05.11.13	708	240	221	247	9

Parade of sail.

Auckland Open Day.

Photo: Marcin Dobrowolski

Even Jon the Mate got his face painted.

Leaving Auckland.

Photo: Sophie Langridge

David Cole

Voyage 23 – Wellington to Nelson by Captain Barbara Campbell

On Friday 8th November, fog at Wellington airport disrupted the joining arrangements for several of the VC. Luckily, by breakfast the following morning, we had caught up with the pre-voyage training.

We cleared the large bay at Wellington shortly after lunch and at 1300 called 'All Hands' for setting sail. The brisk SE winds were due to die away and I wanted to take full advantage of those following winds. Late afternoon the tide turned against us and when the wind fell light after dinner, we clewed up sail and motored to the north, in readiness for the NW wind which was due to pick up after midnight.

The NW wind slowly filled in and at 0400 on the 10th we braced the yards, set sail and headed towards the northern entrance of Queen Charlotte Sound. We passed Motuara Island and Ship's Cove (of Captain Cook fame) around 0730, but soon had to start the engines in addition to the sails to keep the speed up. Two coastguard inflatables and a few local boats

accompanied us from breakfast as a mini-flotilla, and we kept sail set for as long as possible. At 1100, as we approached the port of Picton, we played the Last Post over the tannoy and had two minutes of silence to mark Remembrance Sunday. By 1200 we were all fast alongside No 3 berth. We had a warm welcome from the Edwin Fox museum staff and local supporter Stuart Eyes. The afternoon was hectic, with the ship open to groups with disabilities from 1330 to 1500, and to the general public from 1500 to 1700. About twenty local people in wheelchairs came on board and we were kept very busy. The 'Edwin Fox' museum kept its doors open in the evening for us to have a look around; it was a brilliant hull to visit. Built in 1953, she had been a barque carrying all manner of cargoes as a merchant ship, and is the world's last surviving East Indiaman. In fact, she is the last surviving ship to have carried both immigrants to New Zealand and convicts to Australia.

Assisted climbs started straight after breakfast on 11th, and by 1100 the crew were free to go ashore prior to

Photo: Amy

our departure. The wind increased all morning with gusts of up to 30 knots. With the wind not forecast to decrease for at least 36 hours, we decided to sail to a sheltered location in Queen Charlotte Sound. A coastguard inflatable stood by to help push and a local work boat was made fast to our port bow. Using the wind to push us astern, we slid astern clear of the berth. It never looked an easy manoeuvre and, once clear of the berth, my intention was to continue going astern out of the harbour. However, a big blast of wind came through at the critical moment which pushed the bow round. The work boat was completely ineffective and unable to slip its line, which meant that the coastguard vessel could not come and push. We ended up going sideways out of the harbour, resulting in the merest of glances (but no damage) to an old live-aboard yacht. Once clear we set sails. Bursts of strong winds funnelled down the many inlets. We sailed as much as we could and, at 1700, clewed up sail as we approached Endeavour Inlet. We dragged at our first anchorage off Furneaux Lodge, so we weighed anchor to re-anchor a few miles further off Punga Cove. By 2000 we were settled down with the wind only occasionally reaching 20 knots.

Punga Cove is a secluded low key resort. I went ashore to do a recce the following morning – a jetty allowed most crew to land, but a beach landing was required for those in wheelchairs. Some crew sat in the café by the jetty, others walked a section of the Queen Charlotte

track, or went for a swim. There was occasional drizzle but, by 1600 when we weighed anchor, a few glimpses of blue had crept into the sky. The forecast was for continuing 40 knot SSE'ly winds, but they were due to die out by midnight, ideal for heading west round Stephens Island. We set sail at 1700 and passed Ship Cove in 30 knots of wind from the SSE. After dinner we braced the yards and under just Topsails and Inner Jib, made 7 knots. The seas were following so we rolled at times, but the motion was fine. We rounded Stephens Island, to the north of D'Urville Island, at midnight and continued westwards at 5 knots.

By breakfast the sun was shining as we crossed lovely Golden Bay in 10 to 12 knots of wind. We continued to sail sedately until 1600 when we handed sail and motored a few miles to an anchorage in Wainui Bay. Most crew took advantage of the cool but sunny day. The engineers had a big success with their fishing, catching two good-sized barracuda-type fish.

Dramatic evening at sea.

Photo: Marcin Dobrowolski

We took the voyage photo after breakfast on the 14th then weighed anchor. During Happy Hour we motored east, clear of the coast. The wind was light so we set all the sails and put the boat in the water to take photos. During the afternoon the wind continued to pick up, giving us a good sail. All hands were called at 1500 to hand sail, and at 1640 we anchored inside Tonga Island, off the Abel Tasman coast. The anchorage was stunning and the location idyllic, with the Abel Tasman track just the other side of the beach. A few walkers and kayakers camped behind the beach and the crew were looking forward to going ashore.

After breakfast we put a Harbour Stow in the Fore Course. Whilst this was happening, the DOTI boat and ladder were rigged. Packed lunches were ready and the crew were ferried ashore. Most crew headed off on the boardwalk and over the track to Awaroa lodge with the promise of another lunch, a beer or a coffee. Mark and Otis in wheelchairs did amazingly well; they wheeled themselves along the boardwalk and on to the Abel Tasman track. Through their own endeavours, plus great efforts from 2nd Mate Jim plus other crew members with ropes, they made the 50 minute hike to Awaroa Lodge. The guys in wheelchairs were completely done in, so we paid for them to return to the ship by water taxi, a five mile journey by sea. The water taxi staff did not tell us that the taxi was not allowed to land on the beach by the ship; they could only use the beach round the corner. By this stage I was back on board and it was clear the water taxi could not come alongside *Lord Nelson* either. They shouted "what shall we do with your guys in wheelchairs?" I replied "land them on whichever beach you can". They were no doubt bemused. It is not often that a water taxi leaves two guys in wheelchairs high and dry on a deserted beach. We soon ran the boat in to pick them up. All the crew were back on board for 1800 when we had sun-downers followed by a BBQ. The engineers, cook and various helpers did really well and the evening was a big success.

Photo: Tobias Miller

Following happy hour on the 16th we set sail. However, the light NE'ly wind faded a little, so we made our way to Nelson for a 1500 pilot under sails and one engine. The tide ran across the entrance, so the approach to our berth at Wakefield Quay was not straightforward. We attracted a good slice of the local population for our arrival and had a traditional Maori welcome from a local Maori leader, accompanied by good Maori singing, courtesy of the local primary school. The Sea Cadets were standing to attention in their smart uniforms and the Mayors of both Nelson and Tasman were also there to greet us. Tradition has it that we, in return, had to sing a song! I had found this out first thing that morning so we managed to cobble together a song; "Bring back, bring back, oh bring back Auld Nellie to me, to me"! The school children soon got the hang of the chorus! We showed 20 officials around the ship before the crew went ashore for either a meal or a drink and enjoyed a good night.

Going ashore in the doti boat.

Photo: Amy

On 17th November, following a final Happy Hour, we had bacon butties, then the Captain's de-brief and sign-off. A very happy crew left the ship. Everyone had had a great time. No great distances were covered, but we sailed for 56% of the time and 51% of the distance. This was never going to be a long distance voyage. Had we sailed past Farewell Spit, we would never have got back! Most crew were absolutely delighted that they had chosen this voyage with so many port stops. As so often, we had a great VC, who said they felt the PC were very patient, with a great team spirit, and that we encouraged a good feeling of inclusivity.

Wellington to Nelson by Philippa (Pip) Williams

Our story comes from Philippa (Pip) Williams who sailed alongside the Woodside family on the Wellington to Nelson voyage on *Lord Nelson* in November….

Rolling over in the sun, I turn and ask Andy if he was nervous about going aloft. A few seconds pass, before his lopsided, sunny grin breaks through, and he shakes his head erratically: "Nup." His father, leaning against a pin rail and backlit by the blue Tasman waters, ruefully admits "I've never liked heights. But it was a real moment."

Andy on the helm.

We are on board the *Lord Nelson*, a square rigged sail training ship operated by the Jubilee Sailing Trust (JST). The JST is a British based charity that strives to promote sailing as an activity open to everyone, regardless of an individual's physical capacity. Andy, Alan and myself have all signed up as voyage crew for one leg of Nellie's world circumnavigation – and we are all enjoying ourselves immensely.

A few days prior, Andy had been one of three wheelchair users who chose to make an 'assisted climb'. He went aloft – wheelchair and all – in a harness designed to be hoisted by his fellow crew members. Andy, who grew up an active and sportive child, had not believed that climbing the rigging of a tall ship was within the

range of his possible activities – until he came aboard. Progressive MS has sapped his physical strength, and he relies on the full time care of his parents – Alan and Anne. However, at sea, the Woodside family are crew, standing watch, helming, taking time off ashore, learning lines, cleaning and working in the galley. For what Andy cannot do, the rest of his watch cheerfully steps in, and takes up the slack. In turn, Andy has demonstrated himself as a particularly astute and keen helmsman.

Andy ready to be hoisted aloft.

His parents are immensely proud – both of their son's achievement, and that his achievement had been made possible through the support and kindness of twenty or so other crew members; "complete strangers! All focused on, and so happy for, our son."

Andy is just one of several individuals who make up the complement of the *Lord Nelson's* crew. Up to half of the voyage crew of 40 people may be physically disabled, and the ship can accommodate eight wheelchair users at any one time. Yet, though the *Lord Nelson* is famed as one of two tall ships specifically designed with wheelchair users in mind, its mission is both broader and more grounded than this characterisation may indicate.

At 79, Kay is one of the oldest crew members on board, and she brings with her a lifetime's worth of nautical expertise. Would she, I press, consider arthritis, loss of eyesight, physical frailty and general advancing age, all part of a spectrum of lessening physical ability? She pins me to my seat with a sharp look that makes me squirm. "Of course. The opportunities become limited as you age. It's a shame, because old age is a growth industry."

At its foundations, the *Lord Nelson* operates not as a ship that categorises crews as disabled or abled, but as a contemporary tall ship that actively strives to provide the experience of square rigger sailing to as many people as it can safely and consistently achieve. Further, it is constantly pushing its own definitions of competency, ability and what it means to be a sailor, at roughly the same rate that its varied crew encounter, and overcome, the challenges found at sea.

So when crew are welcomed aboard, they come to Nellie with the understanding that – sitting or standing – we are all subject to the human condition. For each of us, this may mean a different thing: some will be terribly anxious about climbing, whilst others will find the interrupted sleep patterns and close quarters quite an adjustment. Seasickness – though not particularly prevalent on the voyage from Wellington to Nelson – is a universal leveller, and can strike regardless of your age, gender, able-bodied capacity or sea miles traversed.

However, what truly set my time apart on the *Lord Nelson* was the absolute joy that all crew – professional and voluntary, able bodied and physically challenged – took to their time at sea.

Anchored off the Abel Tasman Coast.

Note From Alan Fisher

Sam, the Cook's Assistant on this voyage, contacted me to give me the very sad news that Andy had passed away on 19th January 2016, aged 33 years, after battling with MS for 10 years. I contacted his parents Alan and Anne, and received the following message from Alan:

"Hello Alan. Many thanks for your contact and your condolences. We would be very pleased to have Andy remembered in the passing on of his story, and also for you to mention his own passing. It's part of the story of the work the Trust does, isn't it?"

Dates		Distances in Nautical Miles				Maximum Wind Force
Start	End	Total	Under Sail	Motor-Sailing	Motoring	
08.11.13	17.11.13	295	150	39	106	8

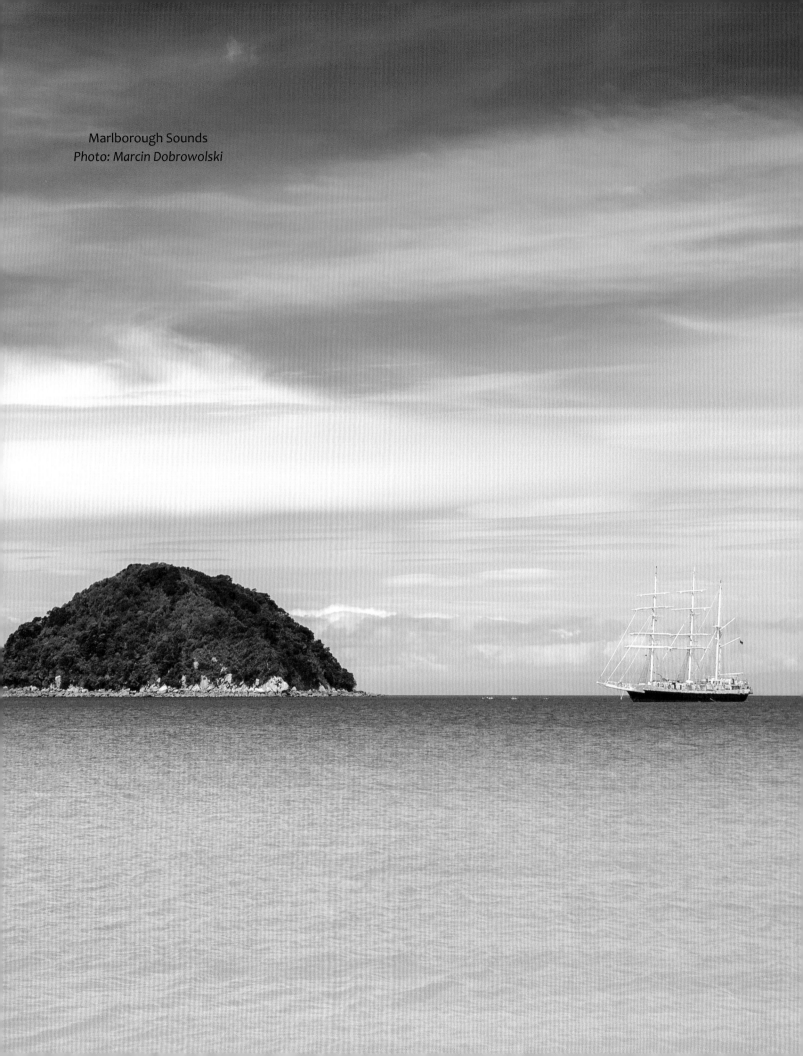

Marlborough Sounds
Photo: Marcin Dobrowolski

Voyage 24 – Nelson to Auckland by Captain Barbara Campbell

The 18th November, joining day, was a cold wet day and 'Hands Aloft' was carried out wearing waterproofs. During the previous voyage, the end of the oil dip-stick in the port main engine broke off in the sump. When the sump was opened up to retrieve it, the gasket fell apart and a new one was to be couriered to us. We delayed sailing to allow time for the engineers to replace the new gasket, and sailed at 1330. The forecast SE'ly wind lay to the north of us; we reached it just before 1800 when we set Topsails and Outer Jib. After dinner T'Gallants and Fore Course were added, giving us a pleasant overnight sail northwards.

Many miles lay between us and Auckland, and going west about North Island was the shortest route, which promised us the best sailing winds. We made good speed under sail until mid-morning when the wind dropped and our speed fell to 2 knots. We clewed up sail after lunch and motored past Mt Taranaki. The mountain remained shrouded in cloud until after dinner, when the cloud lifted and we saw the stunning snow-topped peak. Jumping dolphins and seals close by kept the crew amused. On this voyage we only had time for one port stop and our crew were not the strongest for five straight nights at sea. We timed our arrival off Gannet Island for 0900 to allow a spot of sight-seeing before setting sail. We set all the square sails but the 10 knot easterly wind soon dropped to 5 knots. We sailed on and off which was very frustrating. At least the day was sunny and calm.

The following day the winds were light; some of the time we needed one engine in addition to the sails to make more than 2 or 3 knots. We managed to stop the engine for the morning, sailing along at 3 knots under all square sail and Spanker. Over lunch the wind fell light and we used the starboard engine for two hours. The promised wind finally filled in during the afternoon, and at 1430 we squared the yards, stopped the engine and sailed overnight.

At 0720 on the 23rd, engines were needed in the light ESE'ly winds. We harbour-stowed the Main Course and Spanker and motor-sailed for the day, handing the sails late afternoon. At 1620 we rounded Cape Reinga and motored into a moderate E'ly swell. This was the first real motion that this crew had felt, and a number soon succumbed to mal-de-mer. At 2100 we rounded North Cape, the true north end of North Island, and altered to a SE course.

Bay of Islands.

Following an uncomfortable night motoring into the moderate SE swell, we entered the 'Bay of Islands' about 0930 on the 24th. The area was truly stunning. Those who had been unwell slowly came back to life. The wharf at Opua remains unchanged from the 1960s, though the guy who runs the local store has

become very enterprising by also selling pizzas, beer and coffees. Most of the crew and BMs headed off to find somewhere to lie on a beach. The PC worked till afternoon smoko when some of us went for a late afternoon walk. The local yacht club made us all very welcome for an evening meal; it was a great place to be.

Opua in beautiful Bay of Islands.

The next morning started with the voyage photo and assisted climbs before shore leave. The wind picked up all day from the north so we turned off the berth and motored into the Bay of Islands and set sail for Cape Brett. Unfortunately, the wind fell light at midnight so we handed sails and started the engines, motoring towards Auckland.

Despite having stowed the Main Course and Spanker, we still had four sails to stow. These, together with Happy hour and a Watch Leader debrief took up most of the day. We were off our berth at Princes Wharf West by 1530 and proceeded stern-first to a pontoon next to the berth used by *Spirit of New Zealand*. We rigged a stern gangway to the pontoon and the crew were keen to get ashore for a meal and a drink.

Packing, Happy Hour, bacon butties, the Captain's debrief and payment of bar bills took until 1030 on the 27th, when the crew were free to leave. They had had a great trip and many favourable comments were made in the Watch Leader debrief.

The voyage should have been a day longer as with a total of nine nights on board, six of them were spent at sea. The crew would have loved a BBQ or sundowners, but beyond the one night in Opua, we had no time for an anchorage or another stop. The crew had a great time and though we tried our hardest to sail as much as possible, we only achieved 33% of the time under sail alone.

Manoeuvring in Nelson.

Dates		Distances in Nautical Miles				Maximum Wind Force
Start	End	Total	Under Sail	Motor-Sailing	Motoring	
18.11.13	27.11.13	711	212	224	275	5

Mount Taranaki.
Photo: Liz Turner

Voyage 25 – Auckland to Auckland by Captain Barbara Campbell

The forecast for this voyage was not good, with NW gales already blowing to the south of us, and strong NW winds due to pick up all the way down the east coast of North Island by midnight the following day. So the sensible option was to sail the evening of joining day. We left Princes Wharf in Auckland just after 1830 with the crew of *Spirit of New Zealand* letting our lines go. We went straight into bracing practice and followed this by setting Topsails. By 2000 we were just north of Auckland harbour, under sail and with engines off. We knew the favourable wind would not last and three hours later we clewed up the Topsails and started engines.

At 0400 on 29th, the Topsails were re-set (in readiness for this we had kept the Topsail yards hoisted) and the engines turned off. The Mate managed to set the Fore Course with the 4 to 8 watch and we added all the squares, bar the Main Course, before smoko. After lunch we clewed up sail so that we could motor towards Cape Brett and Bay of Islands. Quiet time was a brief

two hours, followed by a sail setting talk, bracing the yards and a sea stow in a NW force 5, which had slowly built up. We rounded Cape Brett at 2015, and then motored towards an anchorage in Rangihoua Bay. The anchor was let go at 2226 and we enjoyed a sheltered night at anchor.

On 30th, following instruction, we sailed off the anchor just before 1000 and soon made 6 knots south towards Opua. With 25 knots of wind behind us and a flood tide, I decided it would be prudent to let the anchor go and use it to turn the ship into the tide and wind. Despite the channel being narrow, it went well and we soon weighed anchor and then ferry-glided alongside the wooden jetty. Opua may be small, but once again we were made very welcome. After a late lunch the crew either went ashore or took the opportunity for a sleep. In the evening every single member of VC, plus most PC, went ashore to the Opua Cruising Club for a meal and a fun evening.

Following the photograph and assisted climbs the next morning, the crew were free to go ashore. Some sailed on the *R Tucker Thompson*, others rented kayaks, walked, swam, caught the ferry to Russell or wrote postcards. In the evening nearly everyone ate at the Cruising Club for a second night.

In order to be away from the berth before the ebb tide became strong on the 2nd December, we got underway before breakfast, followed by bacon butties on deck. Everyone enjoyed the scenery as we motored slowly towards Roberton Island. We let go anchor shortly before 1000. Roberton Island looked and proved to be stunning. There was good safe swimming in the sandy bay or in one of the two sea-water lagoons. A ten minute walk up hill took you to a Maori Pa with brilliant views in all directions. The crew took packed lunches as the island is largely private, with few dwellings, one of which was home to Captain Jim Cottier and his wife Terri, from *Soren Larsen*. In the evening we had Caiparinhas and a BBQ, with all the PC helping out.

Bay of Islands.

The promised rain and increased E'ly wind arrived promptly the next morning. We sailed off the anchor and clear of the island. We ran out of sea room and had to wear ship at 1140 and again at 1330. We then anchored in Rangihoua Bay undersail, without even starting the engines. This was the bay we had previously anchored in on 29 November. Late afternoon we had a shop, followed by a quiz in the evening.

Overnight the rain was torrential. Faced with a bumpy passage ahead, we had happy hour before departing. After weighing anchor we motored into the wind, making just 4 knots, to round Cape Brett at 1330. At Cape Brett we set fore and aft sail and at 1600 we were in a position to call all hands to set square sails. The wind was NE'ly force 6 so we were soon making 6 knots under Topsails and Fore Course. The swell was running at a height of 3 metres and most of the crew loved sailing in those big seas.

Hauling the main staysail sheet.

At midnight we handed the Fore Course and at 0200 we clewed up the Main Topsail, with the aim of slowing down. We entered the buoyed channel for Auckland at 1030 and remained under sail until 1300, when we started engines. We reversed onto the pontoon which *Spirit of New Zealand* had very kindly lent us. By 1530 the gangway was rigged and the crew allowed ashore. All the VC ate ashore, with several of the PC joining them.

On Friday 6th December a very happy crew departed the ship, most vowing to come back. This had been a brilliant trip with something for everybody. We sailed almost 60% of the total distance, visiting Opua and the delightful Roberton Island. We sailed off the anchor twice, wore ship twice and anchored under sail; all things that VC love to do. The crew all joined in fully, making this a great voyage.

Auckland to Auckland by Diana McLennan

The last 24 hours has seen me clock up several firsts: joining the crew on a Tall Ship, climbing up the mast while the ship was tied up, getting up at midnight to do a "watch" till 4am, "sweating and tailing" the sheets to put out the sails, swabbing the decks (I kid you not, photos to prove) but the most stressing was having to make do with instant coffee at "smoko"!

So, am I OK and am I enjoying it? So far I have to admit to being overwhelmed. Firstly by the closeness of the quarters. The bunk, a narrow, surprisingly comfortable cubicle with minimum amount of storage, but as it is your very own private area it is sacred. Our women's area contains nine curtained cubicles. While working together in groups, especially setting the sails, we are all on top of each other heaving and pulling (like puppies in a basket). The decks are the place to hang out if you need solitude, but there are few limited sitting areas, which are certainly not designed for comfort.

Sailing through the night our first "watch" 12-4am was for me a biggie as I am a legend for my bed rest. This trip may break that belief system! There is definitely something primal about taking a watch in the dead of night with complete darkness all around except for the stars; the cold and wind a reminder that we are such small vulnerable creatures.

Seasickness is about, happily not for me so far, thanks to the 'scopaderm patches'.

I must mention the mast climb. Decided it would be better if I did it while stationary in port; good decision, as to do it when the ship is rocking and rolling ain't my bag. As it was I was hyperventilating with fear, especially the last bit as you have to lean back in a tricky manoeuvre to get onto the platform, and then back down! The marvellous view escaped me as I was too overcome to enjoy it.

Leaving the dock at about 7pm after much safety and sailing instruction we were off under power, headed for Bay of Islands. We sailed/motored all night as the

Aloft in Auckland.

Photo: Dave McIntosh

captain wanted to avoid the weather that was brewing further south. It worked, as we woke (I use that term loosely) to brilliant sunshine and good sailing. It's a great feeling when under sail; the down side is that it means all hands on deck hauling and tailing. Thank goodness I bought some Voltarin.

There are 49 people on board, 9 permanent crew, and 40 of us voyage crew with about 50/50 men and women. The *Lord Nelson* is specifically designed to accommodate disabled crew; one older guy in a wheelchair, an autistic young man with his mum, a beautiful young blind girl, one or two deaf and another with one leg. Without doubt I am the least experienced, but there is always someone giving instruction. Understanding it is my problem. Most of the people have flown in from the UK, the USA and OZ, with only a couple of Kiwis. We are divided into 'watch' groups of eight plus a leader.

Destination Opua. Sailing all night we arrive 12 miles out of Opua ready to dock in the morning; a slow, ponderous manoeuvre with us all on deck manning the sails, sheets and anchor. A miraculous feat of sailing and we are alongside. This has taken all the morning, plus 'happy hour' which is not as we know it, but an hour cleaning the entire ship, above decks and below.

This little ritual happens most days at sea; another good reason to have Voltarin on hand!

We disembark mid-afternoon; because I have local knowledge I appointed myself tour leader. Our group was whisked off in a taxi bus to Pahia, and then walked to Waitangi and did the Treaty House with guided tour. They loved it, and we intend going to Russell tomorrow.

One of the more interesting people on board is Neville, a 16 year-old beautiful Maori boy from south Auckland. He is one of seven children, an art student in Maori cultural art, who won a scholarship place on the ship. He admitted to never having been anywhere out of Manurewa, and he loved going to Waitangi. What an eye opener for him! I suspect he is a space worth watching. He has a quiet reserve and grace which I admire, as he is so out of his comfort zone.

This morning in Opua was a very moving experience. It was the turn of the disabled people to have an assisted climb up the mast. First the chap in the wheelchair, who I learnt has Motor Neuron Disease, a horribly disabling condition that is relentless in its destruction of muscles and movement. With the physical support of one of the Bosuns he made it to the top, an extraordinary feat of courage and trust, followed by Jess, the totally blind 17-year old. She had a grin a mile wide as she was helped aloft. She confided in me later that climbing the mast was the most exciting thing she has ever done. So

humbling, watching these people overcome their fears and putting their trust in another's hands, literally.

It can feel like the top of the world.

Photo: Amy Burns

Off to Russell, again me leading the charge, and a fun time scoping the shops and a climb to the flagpole. Russell has upped its game since last I was there, and the civic pride and attention to the upkeep of the heritage buildings is very impressive. I was proud and impressed.

Food is hearty and plentiful, served in the mess (dining room) by the "mess men" who for that period of time wait on us hand and foot; quite hilarious at times, as we are all crammed in like sardines. Breakfast is served at 8am, so up at 7.30 unless your watch team is on an early shift. Because of the staggered shifts all through the night there are always snuffling and shuffling sounds in the dorm, but I am now well used to it and sleeping very well.

We cast off from Opua at 7.30pm and motored to Robertson Island for a picnic day ashore; great fun and near perfect weather conditions. Again a feeling of pride as the visitors (non Kiwis) were all oohs and arhhs at the beauty that is Bay of Islands. Joy of joys, a pod of dolphins cruised in to the bay swimming in the shallows at thigh high. Some people were in the water with them; there were about twenty of them and they were out to play, giving us a display of diving, jumping and back somersaults. Tonight is a barbecue on deck, and caiparinhas.

I am feeling more confident and "enjoying" the different experiences, bonding with a few people and hopefully adding value where I can. As always with groups, it is about the time when the personality clashes and cracks begin to show.

We wake to rain, unbelievable after the "cracker" day yesterday. The plan is to sail off our moorings and go sailing. As we negotiate our way with "all hands on deck", it is rough and wet. Seasickness is rearing itself again, but not with me. Scarily the prediction is that it will be like this for the rest of the journey. This voyage is no trumped-up experience for the punters. It's the real thing, and that becomes abundantly clear while changing sails in the wind and rain. Not to mention the "bold and heroic" group of people who are up the mast tying and untying sails in full wet weather gear!

Wednesday morning, and as we are rounding Cape Brett the predicted rough weather is upon us. As I write we are in the roughest seas I have been in. On deck, attired in our full wet weather gear and attending to the sails, we are clipped on, staggering about from side to side. The true sailors love it; I feel quite safe and, unlike some of the people, I am not sick (yet), however I have to own being a bit of a "Margot" as I move around. Down in the mess things that are not tied down are flying about, including us. I am going to my nest to escape till my next duty.

Our group is on the 6-8pm watch, so in the pouring rain and wind, we stare out to sea for two hours, one of us on the helm. We are sailing through the night towards Auckland, the rough weather is so tiring, staggering about from one hand-hold to the next, negotiating the steep stairs to the mess and the accommodation. Have taken a seasick pill, just in case.

We wake to more torrential rain and wind after a bumpy night. I am now sick of it, BUT we are on the 8-12am watch; we don our wet weather gear and stand on watch as we approach the channel, tying up at the quay about 2pm......, yet another feat of nautical manoeuvring. Disappointing, as I had had the romantic notion of us sailing into the harbour with all sails up, instead of sliding in under power shrouded in weather. The statistics of the voyage: we were under sail 59% of the time and covered 306 miles.

A shag, drying its wings.

So what are my overall impressions? It definitely will be a oncer for me. It's not that I haven't enjoyed it, but "enjoy" is probably too strong a word. The whole trip was an experience out of my comfort zones, challenging, in particular my physicality and tolerance to withstand the close quarters with people from all over and all walks of life. The common factor was that we all share an adventurous spirit. Several are continuing on for the 60-day voyage to South America with no stops.

NOT ME!!!.

Dates		Distances in Nautical Miles				Maximum Wind Force
Start	End	Total	Under Sail	Motor-Sailing	Motoring	
28.11.13	06.12.13	306	172	58	76	6

Auckland to Auckland by Sue Tupper Watch Leader

I have always wanted to go to New Zealand but never thought it would be on a tall ship. I was thrilled when Jo Hall said that Watch Leaders were needed for the NZ voyages and would I like to go and stay on for Open Ships PR. Didn't have to think about that one too long! I know we don't have favourites (ships or voyages) but I reckon this has to be right up there. Wonderful weather, scenery, ship, Captain and entire crew. I had a full of watch of ten, none of whom had ever sailed on a tall ship before, and Captain Barbara decided that, in order to get ahead of some nasty weather, we would sail away first night! All four seasons in a day is what Kiwis say about their weather, which was so true – factor 50 sun cream, oilies and ski gear all needed every day. So in the dark, knowing no one's names or abilities, not yet recognising silhouettes, they started to learn to helm the ship and get to know the ropes and each other. Great way to bond. Wonderful friendships were made. One lady, Ruth, who had sailed to accompany her autistic grandson Lachlan on the voyage, even flew to the UK to welcome Nellie home nine months later, and stayed on for another voyage with Caroline from our watch. NZ did appear a lot like Wales to begin with – lots of space, fields, hills and sheep, with a Scandinavian influence thrown in with the wooden houses. A kiwi forester on board told us that many of the native trees have been replaced with European deciduous trees by the settlers so that it looked like the UK, and also conifers have been planted for the production of paper to be exported to China.

Captain Barbara managed to fit in incredible sailing, anchorages in idyllic bays, local fish restaurants, swimming in the warm seas and an insight into the history of NZ. We even found a former Bosun of *Lord Nelson* and Captain of *Soren Larsen*, like Robinson Crusoe, living on remote Roberton Island, where Captain Cook had landed 300 years earlier.

Sailing back to Auckland from the Bay of Islands brought us incredible contrasting experiences, from the picture-perfect blue seas, skies, islands and beaches following Captain Cook's historic footsteps, to exhilarating wild stormy seas tossing Nellie to inclines of 35°. As I helped Lawrie Bassett from my watch off the ship at the end of the voyage, anxious that his wife of 41 years would have read his blog where he told how his wedding ring had had to be cut off (it's a wonderful tale and no, she hadn't), he also told me his middle name was Nelson and that he was a distant relative. He was the second oldest person with MS after Stephen Hawking, and had thoroughly enjoyed his adventure on the ship. Yet another fantastic voyage that proves how small the world is, even though it seems so big that it takes a ship two years to sail around it. We are all connected. The JST certainly lives up to its strapline of 'Changing Lives', for able bodied and disabled voyagers. I love it!

Leg 6

Auckland to Ushuaia by Captain Chris Phillips

How to summarise this voyage? It was the longest continuous sea passage ever undertaken by the Trust's ships, and a real adventure for those of us who had the privilege to undertake it.

I joined the ship after a fantastic month or so of leave travelling the length and breadth of New Zealand, straight into a short maintenance period alongside in Auckland to make the final preparations for this groundbreaking trip. As often happens with such voyages, we suffered a few delays in departure. A main topmast stay needed replacing which was discovered during the maintenance; we had to wait for the new stay to be made up, which involved tools being imported from Australia. We took stores for six weeks or so at sea – the largest Store Ship we have ever done, squeezing provisions into every conceivable corner.

We finally sailed from Auckland a couple of days late, after working long into the previous night to reassemble and send up the new main topmast stay and its furling gear. The sail was bent on at sea as we motored out in calm conditions. We had an unremarkable three-day passage to Napier, where we took fuel on Christmas Eve and enjoyed Christmas Day alongside, whilst Alan, the Chief Engineer, had to find a refrigeration engineer who would come out on Christmas Day to fix the vegetable locker plant. We sailed on Boxing Day, having cleared customs first thing in the morning.

After a mixed passage of motoring and sailing, we reached the remote outpost of the Chatham Islands on 29th December and spent a day on the islands, well looked after by the islanders, and contributing to their funds by betting on the horses during their annual race day.

We moved off the jetty for a more comfortable night at anchor before sailing the following morning, bound for Cape Horn. As we rounded the south of the islands, we encountered a pod of Orca who had obviously come to wave us off.

The next 34 days saw us sailing along the 45th parallel in a variety of conditions, but none too scary, before dipping down to the latitude of Cape Horn. We crossed the dateline at New Year, so added an extra day to December and celebrated New Year's Eve two nights running. The crew entertained themselves in a variety of ways – the old standards of the Murder Game, the Egg Drop, quizzes, talks, shanty and poetry sessions all featured in our repertoire, as well as the nightly instalments of our own soap opera, "Horatio and Chardonnay" during the Captain's evening broadcast.

We drilled in abandon ship procedures and reefing the Fore Topsail, as well as compulsory viewing of Irving Johnson's Cape Horn video (somehow interpreted one evening as a "Gay Porn" video – they do sound slightly alike, I suppose) in anticipation of the conditions we might face in those notorious waters, but in the event we were becalmed off the Horn for nigh on 24 hours, and held a Man Overboard drill, followed by a photocall both from the boat and on board.

Modelling the latest Southern Ocean fashion!

Photo: Barbara Box

Once round the Horn, our mission was to continue sailing north up the east coast to 50° south, so as to qualify the whole crew for membership of the International Association of Cape Horners. In the event, we reached 51° 22'S before wind and time turned against us, but this was deemed sufficient by the Association to grant us membership. From there we motored and sailed back to the south and into the Beagle Channel, reaching Ushuaia having spent the last 41 days at sea since leaving the Chathams.

Steve Higgs and Paul Moorby.

Cape Horn
Photo: Marcin Dobrowolski

Auckland to Ushuaia by Brian Bowell

Between December 2013 and February 2014 the *STS Lord Nelson* sailed from Auckland to Ushuaia round Cape Horn, with 47 souls on board. I was one of those 47 and this is my story.

At the outset I should say I'm no yachty. A trip cross-channel many years ago had me curled up in the stern while my wife made the bacon sandwiches. A move to New Zealand found me introduced to the *Soren Larsen*, and the joys of tall ship sailing in the South Pacific. Three voyages later and the *HMB Endeavour* announced its circumnavigation of Australia. I signed on for the first and last legs and was proud to be on the helm as we sailed into Sydney harbour.

But these were shortish trips and I wanted a more substantial voyage, but they are not easy to find down here. My sea-going mate, Sean, sent me details of the *Lord Nelson* and its circumnavigation, including the Holy Grail – Round the Horn. Within 48 hours I'd signed up and passed over the deposit. All I needed then was the balance and an airfare home from Ushuaia. As the time approached I watched her progress round the world and read the voyage blogs. I practised knots and hitches, and read about the likely progress of the voyage. I had Jim Cottier's book about the *Soren Larsen's* rounding for background. Eventually departure day, December 15th, came around and I found myself at Viaduct Basin, saying farewell to my family and going aboard.

What followed was an avalanche of introductions, instructions, information, names, faces and places on board. The master, Captain Phillips, (no, not that Captain Phillips) made himself known and explained 'The Plan'. *Lord Nelson* has roller-furling sails and the furling mechanism for the Main Staysail had failed and there was a problem with the Fore TopGallant, which meant that manual furling was needed. The staysail furling gear was obsolete, and its repair involved engineers in New Zealand and Australia. So 'The Plan' was to get it fixed ASAP, whilst stores for the six-week

passage were delivered and stowed and we got to know each other and the ship. It was the 19th before the repair was done and signed off, so we could leave on the 20th for Napier on the East coast, a shakedown voyage of about 350 nautical miles, and a last chance to take on fuel and water. There we would celebrate Christmas before leaving for the Chatham Islands, an outpost of NZ, about another 450M to the east.

Christmas Dinner alongside in Napier.

Photo: Natalie Osborne

The voyage to Napier was uneventful. We all got used to sea watches and sail handling on deck and aloft. We were alongside Napier dock on the evening of December 23rd. Christmas came and went with a full celebration on board, swimming for some hardier than me, and calls home. Chef Dave Stanley and his colleagues produced a traditional Christmas dinner, served to the voyage crew by the captain and his officers. Boxing Day saw us up and away on the second leg, to the Chatham Islands. These are a group of four islands and smaller outcroppings some 850km east of the mainland. Only two of the islands, Pitt and Chatham, are inhabited.

First-timers had their first taste of swells and the motion of the ship in heavy weather on this leg. Although seasickness was fairly contained, the looks on faces at the first breakers over the deck were priceless. Netting was laid alongside the sides of the deck – 'Sailor Strainers', enquirers were told. Early on the morning of the 29th we were off the jetty at Chatham and, after some difficulty, were moored. We were all given shore leave on the proviso that we kept a weather eye out for a warning flag to signal all hands on board.

The crew enjoyed a variety of pursuits. There is a small store and post office, together with a hotel near the jetty. Several of the voyage crew spent the day in ornithological pursuits, and most of the rest of us spent a day at the races. It was Chatham's Christmas race day with trotting and flat racing events, accompanied by Speights beer and pies. Late in the afternoon the signal flag was seen aloft and we all made our way back on board. An offshore wind was pushing the ship onto the jetty, so all hands were needed to move her to a safe anchorage offshore. The next day, the 30th, we hoisted sail and left Chatham on the long passage east to Cape Horn.

The route established by trading ships voyaging from Australia to the U.K. was known as the Great Circle Route, and took them well down to latitude south 65° and beyond. Captain Phillips's plan was more conservative. Not wanting to risk the ship (and us) to the perils of ice and severe weather, he planned a route that would keep us north of the worst of the weather and any floating ice masses. That actually meant that we varied our course to take best advantage of the winds, and also kept our engines silenced. A waypoint 56°S & 63°W to the east of Cape Horn was our target. As the winds veered, our generally eastwards passage was marked by deviation north or south in order to make the best of what wind was available. Daily progress varied; on a good day we made 170 miles, on a slack day less than 100. Whilst helming one evening, our watch, Port Aft, recorded a speed of 0 knots and 0 miles progress in the hour. An achievement the following watch tried to better.

So we progressed across the South Pacific, accompanied by waves and albatrosses, our daily routine established. No other shipping on our radar, and a great dark

Skimming albatross.

immensity below and around us. I enjoy tall ship voyaging as a job of work. I get up, dress up and show up to do what's needed to push this small colony across the ocean. There is a routine within a routine. The watches rotate and the ship has another, daily timetable. We serve as mess men (people) preparing food, laying tables and doing endless washing up. Happy hour each morning sees all four watches either on or below decks keeping the ship clean. Some of us specialise. I cleaned heads.

Voyaging on *Lord Nelson* is not all work. There are leisure options to provide distraction. These included a murder game that involved everyone trying to kill each other in a specific place with a particular weapon. Cluedo goes to Sea! There was an Easter competition involving the launching of eggs from the mainmast fighting top, and of course Wednesday evening Twister in the bar. The bar and library became the social hub of the ship during each evening, and the hourly safety round below decks could be quite prolonged. Every afternoon, one of us gave a talk on some aspect of interest. There were poetry readings and a scratch sea shanty choir. Each evening Captain Phillips reported our progress along with an episode of 'Horatio & Chardonnay' a sea-going saga of on-board romance. Ralph McTell, singing 'Around the Wild Cape Horn', introduced each episode.

Margaret & Neil practising in the engine room for New Year.

Photo: Tracey Watson

My diary for January 10th records: 0400 – 0800 aloft at 4 to remove Fore T'Gallant gaskets. Set the Fore T'Gallant and later Main T 'Gallant. Course 090°, weather cold and damp. On January 13th we arrived at a point the furthest from any land in any direction, a sobering thought that took me back to 1981 and that channel crossing. Burns night, January 25th, had us celebrating with Haggis and Cranachan, along with toasts to the bard and recitations. It was also significant as the day we sailed into the Southern Ocean at 50°S, less than 1000 miles from Cape Horn. Then on January 31st: there are rumours of land. It's out there, but obscured by cloud. The next day, February 1st: Cape Horn is off the port bow, a few miles away. It's now 33 days (we had New Year's Eve twice). Most sails are handed and we sail slowly along. The *Soren Larsen's* IACH flag hangs from the main mast. Gasketed the Spanker.

The next few days were almost an anti-climax. To comply with IACH requirements we needed to sail up the east coast of Argentina and so cross 50° of latitude both east and west of Cape Horn. Then, on February 6th, we turned back and started the engine for the journey back to the Beagle Channel. During this time we went through a harbour stow and gave the ship a good cleaning. On February 9th we collected the

pilot and spent the day motor sailing up the channel to Ushuaia and the voyage end. 3 pm saw us moored alongside modern cruise ships, fishing boats and *Europa*, a Dutch tall ship running trips to Antarctica.

Scrubbing the decks.

The voyage was over. A couple of days were spent on board, cleaning, laying in stores, a harbour watch. There was shore leave and we explored the town along with trips to a glacier and an island with 10,000 penguins living there. Departure day came around and I began the first of three flights home to New Zealand. A journey of almost three months is now made in less than a day. As we fly west over the ocean I remember seeing aircraft lights among the stars on a night in mid-January and wonder if that was the same flight.

Megan taking a 'sight'.

Photo: Marcin Dobrowolski

Would I do it again? You bet I would. I still cherish every moment, and stepped ashore in Ushuaia with pride and sadness. Pride at what I and all of us have made happen, and sadness that we may never be united again.

47 souls on board and all's well.

REFERENCES

Cottier Jim, Captain *Soren Larsen*. Homeward Bound Round The Horn. The Bush Press New Zealand. 1997. ISBN 0-908608-77-2

Ralph McTell. Around the Wild Cape Horn. Album: Somewhere Down the Road, 2010.

What do you think of it so far? A few days into the voyage

Some VC have asked me 'what do you think of it so far?' The voyage I mean.

Well, I'm loving every moment of it. There are times when I feel my heart lifted by the enterprise we are engaged in. There is joy in the rolling sea, in all its colours and motion.

The days pass in a rhythm set by watches, convivial meals and best of all 'Happy Hour'. The bar hums with conversation "it's like a library in here." My companions are pleasant and sociable, but appreciate others' need for space and tolerance. So far I'm not disposed to dispose of anyone.

How shall I describe the journey to people when I'm home again? Neil described it as the Holy Grail of tall ship sailing. My Holy Grail is:

Long periods of inactivity punctuated by bursts of labour, usually at a watch change.

Watching Orion and the Southern Cross wheel across the night sky.

Swaying on the fore T'Gallant yard at 4a.m. as my life flashes before my eyes.

Counting how many rolls of lavatory paper are needed to stock up the heads.

What's for dinner?

How many more miles to the Horn? How many? Surely not.

That's how it is so far for me. How about you?

And now as we near the end of the voyage.

Earlier in this voyage I asked myself 'what do you think of it so far?' Now, as we reach the end of the journey, I'm revisiting the question.

Cape Horn has been reached and rounded, albeit not in the way we might have expected. There were no monumental seas, hurricanes hardly happened and the decks stayed annoyingly dry. We reached and rounded in almost dead calm conditions. A zephyr gently eased us along and some were seen sunbathing. But none the less, the sense of wonder and accomplishment was undiminished. We have done what very few men and women have done in recent years.

We are still a crew united in a common purpose. No mutinies or disputes have riven us, despite 40-odd of us living in each other's pockets. The bar still looks like a library, and I stand watch, lay aloft, chop pumpkins and relish Happy Hour. We have the cleanest fo'c'sle heads in the Southern Hemisphere.

Dates		Distances in Nautical Miles				Maximum Wind Force
Start	End	Total	Under Sail	Motor-Sailing	Motoring	
15.12.13	12.02.14	6429	5418	628	383	9

Voyage 26 – Ushuaia to Ushuaia by Captain Chris Phillips

If the last voyage was an Ultra-Marathon, this was the equivalent of an Ironman endurance event. It was the most challenging voyage I have ever undertaken from many points of view, and it tested the entire crew to their limits.

We were lucky enough to have on board Skip Novak, possibly the most established expert in sailing in Antarctica, who would be acting as advisor and expedition leader. Also, in order to satisfy our regulators in the MCA, we had to carry a couple of extra certificated hands for watchkeeping duties, so we had Kirsten Mackay, an experienced BM but also holder of a Watch Rating certificate, and Piers Alvarez-Munoz, a Master Mariner with plenty of experience in our ships and in the ice.

This was not a voyage for sailing. We had a limited weather window to get south across the Drake Passage, and once in the archipelago around the Peninsula we had to keep our wits about us, but also had either no wind or headwinds the entire time!

Skip joins wheelchair users aloft.

Photo: Skip Novak

Anchorages at Deception Island, Cuverville Island, Port Lockroy and Vernadsky Base in the Argentine Islands served us well, with a constant watch kept for growlers and bergs. We had a number of challenges to overcome, not least that of fresh water conservation and production; short of melting down icebergs there was no readily available source of fresh water to fill the tanks, so we had to come up with imaginative solutions to enable us to use the water maker outside our normal operating parameters. The watch keeping was intense, and not helped by almost the entire crew suffering from a 24-hour stomach upset, meaning that we were shorthanded for several days.

However, it was a genuine adventure, taking all of us and the ship out of our comfort zones; we saw some amazing scenery and wildlife; we met some wonderful people (the Ukrainians at Vernadsky on the eve of the Russian invasion of Ukraine, perhaps taking too much comfort from their home-brewed vodka); we landed possibly the first wheelchair-users on the continent; we learnt that penguins really do smell quite bad; most of all we learnt that down there, the weather is most definitely the boss, illustrated perfectly during the storm we experienced on the northbound passage back to Ushuaia.

Ushuaia to Ushuaia by Katherine Morris

21/2/14 – We visited the desolate and eerie stations on Deception Island, the caldera of an active volcano. I was amazed by the juxtaposition of steam rising from the hot springs into the freezing air.

24/2/14 – I explored Curverville Landing dressed up in my penguin onesie, had several Gentoo chicks look at me with confusion! If you sat still for a few minutes the Gentoo chicks came right up to you. It felt like they were as intrigued by us as we were by them.

28/2/14 – We met Doug Allen, an incredibly talented underwater cameraman who has done a lot of work with David Attenborough and was kind enough to visit us for an evening and share some of his fascinating stories.

3/3/14 – At the Faraday Bar in Vernadsky Research Station, several of us got rather tipsy with the Ukrainians drinking their home-brewed vodka. The snooker table was moved out of the way to make room for dancing, bras were donated and much silliness ensued. The poor BMs had a tough time convincing us to leave!

Kate, blending in with the locals.
Photo: Katherine Morris

Snow sail.

Photo: Skip Novak

Penguins on the rocks!

Photo: Toria Hunt

Is this my best side?

Photo: Toria Hunt

Kate admiring the view astern.

Photo: Sue Hunt

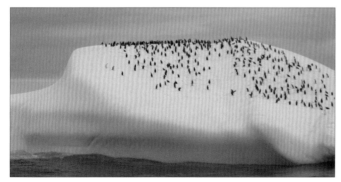

Our first iceberg, home to hundreds of chinstrap penguins

Photo: Barbara Box

Third Officer Lesley and Kirsten getting the boat ready.

Photo: Paul and Kath Ginnever

The following pages are reprinted with the kind permission of Yachting World.

I would be very happy if you would like to reproduce the article in your book, anything we can do to help the charity.

Good luck with the book.

Elaine Bunting
Editor, Yachting World

INTREPID

"Tense and unnerving" is not how you'd expect Skip Novak to describe an Antarctic cruise. But even high-latitudes experts must have a first time, especially when inching along a swaying yard in a Force 7. And three weeks aboard the Jubilee Sailing Trust's 55m barque *Lord Nelson* was always going to be much more than the average expedition

IN THE ICE

LORD NELSON

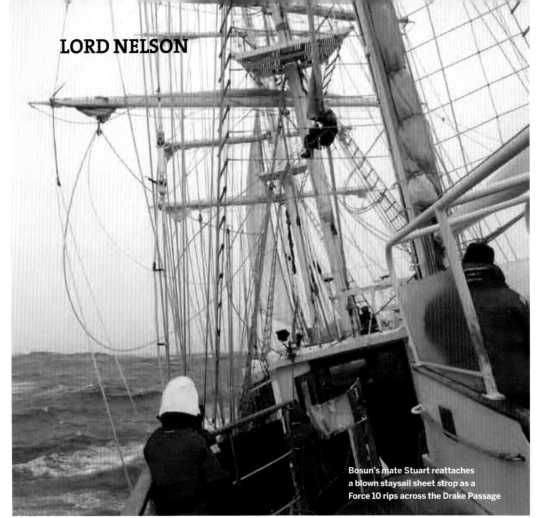

Bosun's mate Stuart reattaches
a blown staysail sheet strop as a
Force 10 rips across the Drake Passage

Captain Chris
Phillips braves
the cold

On watch on the bridge

I'm not one to pass up the opportunity to climb out of my comfort zone. But on 5 March I occasionally questioned my judgment. Just west of the South Shetland Islands in the Antarctic, I found myself in a Force 10 northerly. The barometer had slid to 971mb and the barque *Lord Nelson* was getting it on the nose on our homeward passage to Ushuaia. It had been a memorable morning.

As we clawed off the Shetlands for sea room, the square sails were stowed to leave just 'fore and afters'. First the clew strop on the mizzen staysail parted, followed shortly after by the head strop on the main staysail. Changing from the roller-furling outer jib to the smaller hanked-on inner jib on the bowsprit in a driving snowstorm was a refreshing experience, to put it mildly.

With a single sail forward and both engines going, the ship was holding station comfortably even if those of us on board were not ultimately comfortable. If there's one thing I've learned from sailing the Drake Passage in high winds, it's that a Force 10 is best avoided.

Lord Nelson is a square-rigger operated by the Jubilee Sailing Trust (JST) that, like their second vessel, *Tenacious*, provides a sail training experience for a mix of able-bodied and disabled crew; a unique programme not only in the UK, but worldwide.

She was on the last stages of a two-year, under-publicised tour that had included South Africa, India, Australia and New Zealand before a voyage through the Southern Ocean to Argentina. She would continue home via Brazil and Halifax before arriving in Southampton this September.

From the Chatham Islands off the east coast of New Zealand, she had sailed 34 days to the Beagle Channel without motoring, calms included, and doubled Cape Horn 50°S to 50°S (by continuing up towards the Falklands and back down!) to qualify her crew for the ring in the ear. She was the first British square-rigger to have made this passage since 1991. This is a very capable vessel sailed by a very capable crew.

Working aloft is addictive

With *Lord Nelson* in Ushuaia, I signed on as a supernumerary on 15 February to meet Captain Chris Phillips and his permanent crew. I was to be a pilot and expedition leader for the ship's 25-day cruise to the Antarctic Peninsula, there to cover safety in the ice and anchorages, advise on the itinerary and environmental matters and to conduct visits ashore.

This all came about because I had known John Tanner as a rival navigator in the 1977-78 Whitbread Race. He was on board Clare Francis's *ADC Accutrac* and I was on *King's Legend*. Even though I hadn't seen him since, he had advised his nephew, Captain Chris, a commissioned Royal Naval officer, to contact me for advice.

One thing led to another and once given the nod by Andy Spark, operations manager of the JST and its driving force, I found myself on the end of t'gallant (top gallant) in the Drake Passage three days after signing on board, putting gaskets on the clewed up sail while bowling along on a Southern Ocean swell under topsails alone in a 30-knot westerly.

I am used to working aloft on single masts, but those first few minutes were tense and unnerving. Stuart, a young

Beautiful weather, astonishing scenery – our day at Peterman Island was as good as it gets in Antarctica

❝ Wearing a harness, you are safe when on the yard in theory. Yet falling off on to the safety wire could be ugly – embarrassing at the least ❞

marine biologist and one of the bosun's mates, settled me down with a few tips on how to relax and stay tacked on. I immediately began to enjoy the ride immensely. He warned me that working aloft was addictive, but he had had his 'moments'.

When climbing up the ratlines you are on your own – no change from the days of Jack Aubrey, the fictional captain of Patrick O'Brian's novels. At the top you clip on to a safety wire that leads over the futtock shrouds to the crosstrees. There you clip on to the safety wire along the yard and move out.

So, in theory you are safe. Yet falling off on to the safety wires at any point could be ugly – embarrassing at the very least. Letting go is not really an option.

Lord Nelson carried a complement of 50 people for this voyage. Some 35 were either 'voyage crew' – aged 24 years old to 77, the average age being 57 – or paying trainees who included watch leaders, who had a substantial number of voyages under their belts. The permanent crew of nine included the deck officers, two engineers, a medical purser, a cook and a bosun. Four volunteers were also signed on, designated as bosun's mates and a so-called 'cook's ass' – the word 'assistant' was too long to fit into its allotted cell on the crew spreadsheet!

A few more than normal for this voyage, the volunteers were can-do men and women who knew the ship from previous voyages and did the heavy work. They made ▶

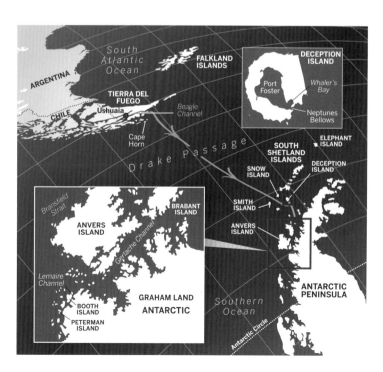

▲ Above (left-right): a group effort helps Croat Mislav, paralysed in the Balkans war, ashore at Port Lockroy; everyone goes on watch

▲ Above (left-right): furling sails in the caldera at Deception Island; the ship is cleaned six days a week during 'Happy Hour' after breakfast

running repairs beyond the capabilities of the voyage crew and were instrumental in providing muscle for landings.

The crew were split into four watches and stood four hours on and eight off. Responsibilities included steering (there is no autopilot), look-outs on either side and a scribe to record log entries and meteorological readings. Bracing the yards and setting fore and after sails required two watches or all hands in heavy weather. Oncoming watches also had to help prepare meals – the amount of work required to scrub and chop potatoes and green beans for 50 cannot be under-estimated – then wash up. Except on Sundays, there was 'Happy Hour' after breakfast – a pull-through from stem to stern to clean the decks, heads and galley no matter what the weather.

Across the Polar Front

We had three wheelchair users on board and several walking wounded. None was excluded from any of these tasks. The rule was they were not to be helped unless they asked for help. So, if you seek rest and relaxation, the JST is not for you. Disabled or not, you come as crew. They take no passengers.

As usual with a Drake Passage crossing, we motorsailed when the wind died between weather systems. The object is to get across and not dally – conditions can only get worse. We passed south of the Antarctic Convergence on 19 February.

This boundary zone, known by scientists as the Polar Front, is where the cold water of the Southern Ocean meets the super-cold water of Antarctica. We were accompanied by a proliferation of black browed and wandering albatross, cape pigeons, Wilson's storm petrels and a plethora of other petrels, unidentifiable to the layman. The water temperature dropped and settled at about 2°C. This zone of upwelling nutrients provides a haven for the Southern Ocean food chain, and its ring around the Antarctic continent isolates this unique polar ecosystem.

Although big bergs can persist for a time north of the Polar Front, once south of 60°S ice was our main concern.

To obtain an Antarctic Permit, *Lord Nelson* had to be considered seaworthy by the Maritime & Coastguard Agency (MCA). That the MCA had approved *Lord Nelson*'s world tour, including the 4,000-mile passage from New Zealand to Cape Horn counted for nothing in a proposed Antarctic voyage, which featured a short stretch of the Drake Passage, then a flexible itinerary within a relatively sheltered archipelago. Concerns were raised regarding stability, the windage of the rig and the strength of the hull in ice. Such is the enigma of bureaucracy.

But with those hurdles cleared and the Drake successfully passed, we made our misty landfalls on Smith and Snow islands then passed through Neptunes Bellows, the entrance to Deception Island. This is the usual first shelter after a Drake

Freezing but fun – a dusting of snow on the inner jib is standard on a cruise of the Antarctic Peninsula

> ❝ If you seek rest and relaxation, the Jubilee Sailing Trust is not for you. Disabled or not, you come as crew. They take no passengers ❞

crossing. It affords an easy landing beach-head and a trip ashore to Whalers Bay inside the drowned caldera of a semi-active volcanic, a unique feature in the Antarctic.

Having given way to a cruise ship that had scheduled an afternoon landing, we came to grips with getting people ashore that evening. The landings were the object of the voyage for me. The attractions were the ruins of the Norwegian whaling station from the 1920s and the remains of a British Antarctic Survey base destroyed by the last volcanic eruption in 1969.

Enter Piers Alvarez-Munos, my colleague, who was seconded to get us through the MCA's hoops. A master mariner and superb raconteur, he had just finished a stint as first mate on the cruise ship *National Geographic Explorer*. Having served on the *Lord Nelson* in her early years, he organised disembarkations and re-embarkations and handled all the tender-driving, leaving me to enjoy myself on shore.

Lord Nelson usually disembarks its crew via a gangway on to jetties. The ship was designed with electric lifts to allow wheelchair users independent access to the three decks, but transferring people into an inflatable tender was another matter.

Actually, disability is a relative thing. Although we had three wheelchair users, things moved slowly anyway given that the average age of the voyage crew pushed 60 and people had to descend a ladder over the side into a heaving tender. The many layers of clothing and lifejackets required sometimes brought the process to a near standstill.

It took an hour and a half to get 40 people ashore, but it was a good first run. There is nothing like a walk (or a wheel) ashore at Deception to cure chronic seasickness from a Drake crossing or relieve lingering anxieties about the voyage. All worries are forgotten once on *terra firma*, at close quarters to a pair of chinstrap penguins which look you up and down or see a fur seal. This is when the Antarctic adventure really begins.

The group enjoyed a very atmospheric time ashore – dull grey conditions gave way to a euphoric burst of sunlight over the caldera rim just before nightfall.

The next day we headed south across the Bransfield Strait and into the Gerlache Straits, dodging bergy bits and growlers on radar and by eye during a dark night. Piers and I were operating six-on, six-off at the end of the bowsprit with a ▶

LORD NELSON

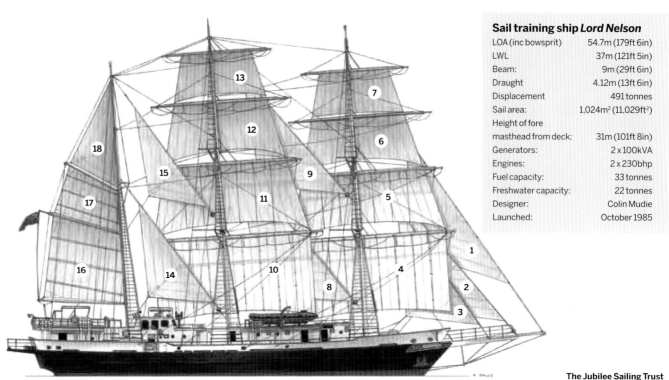

Sail training ship *Lord Nelson*

LOA (inc bowsprit)	54.7m (179ft 6in)
LWL	37m (121ft 5in)
Beam:	9m (29ft 6in)
Draught	4.12m (13ft 6in)
Displacement	491 tonnes
Sail area:	1,024m² (11,029ft²)
Height of fore	
masthead from deck:	31m (101ft 8in)
Generators:	2 x 100kVA
Engines:	2 x 230bhp
Fuel capacity:	33 tonnes
Freshwater capacity:	22 tonnes
Designer:	Colin Mudie
Launched:	October 1985

The Jubilee Sailing Trust ships *Lord Nelson* and *Tenacious* sail 12 months a year and anyone can join a voyage, aged 16 upwards, no sailing experience required. To find out more, visit jst.org.uk

Lord Nelson's sails

1	Flying jib	5	Fore topsail	10	Main course	15	Mizzen t'gallant staysail
2	Outer jib	6	Fore t'gallant	11	Main topsail	16	Spanker
3	Inner jib	7	Fore royal	12	Main t'gallant	17	Upper spanker
4	Fore course	8	Main staysail	13	Main royal	18	Spanker topsail
		9	Main t'gallant staysail	14	Mizzen staysail		

▲ **Above: with over 50 crew on board, cook Derek, a retired fireman, has his work cut out**

▶ **Right: author Skip Novak (left) with Captain Chris and bosun's mate Stuart**

VHF radio and a projector lamp. However, some of the pressure was off. We had arrived on the peninsula.

A cross-section of society

Over the next few weeks we mingled with the penguins and seals onshore and off, observed whales and icebergs, took in the vistas. I met a banking executive, business gurus, healthcare workers, teachers, a geologist, a retired fireman and Royal Navy helicopter pilot, consultants, an IT man and an occupational therapist. It was a cross-section of British society, with a few Irish, a Kiwi, a couple of Aussies and a Croat to mix it up.

Most had been on previous JST voyages, a few as many as 20 times. However, these voyages are not for the over-sensitive – you have to take a ribbing and dish it back out to survive!

Over our 12 days on the peninsula, we made six good landings and spent periods hunkered down at anchor. We failed to go through the Lemaire Channel due to ice blockage twice until we finally got through. The weather was generally windy, closed and hard going, with only one truly stellar day ashore.

Having retreated from trying to pass the Lemaire Channel on 3 March, again due to ice, Captain Chris brought us back into the anchorage in the Argentine Islands in a blinding snowstorm. It was one of the finest pieces of seamanship I had ever witnessed given the conditions and vessel. This was also our last shelter before striking north on the homeward passage.

Just beneath Cape Horn a new 956mb low ripped across and a Force 9 from the south-west drove us under topsails and jib up into the Beagle Channel for an exciting finish before we dropped the hook at the pilot station on 10 March to tidy up.

Most officers and voyage crew admitted this has been one of the most demanding yet most satisfying voyages on 'Nelly'. We were pleasantly exhausted – and isn't that the way a true sea voyage should end? At the captain's debrief, I addressed the crew. I told them the word 'expedition' was one of the most over-used misconstrued words in travel today – everyone on a cruise ship is on some sort of expedition or another, it seems.

Sailing the *Lord Nelson*, a collective effort of 50 people, is very different. Every member of this crew had been on a genuine adventure. I told them if anyone ever asked, they could put their hands on their hearts, and say, yes, they had been on a true sailing expedition. **YW**

Returning home after a long day from Cuverille Island.

Photo: Marcin Dobrosolski

Ice lookouts aloft.

Photo: Marcin Dobrowolski

P.p.p.p ...pick-up a Penguin!

Photo: Marcin Dobrowolski

Ice lookouts on the bow.

Photo: Marcin Dobrowolski

Let go starboard anchor.

Photo: Skip Novak

At anchor in Port Lockroy.

Photo: Tom Smith

A Recollection of a Journey by Dr Louise Crockett

Throughout the passage north I'd been confined in my coffin-shaped bunk in the fo'c'sle. The heads were four hand-holds away, and that was about the limit of my ability to stand upright. Our barque, five-hundred tons of steel, canvas and rope carrying us fifty crew was thrown wildly in the Southern Ocean like a walnut-shell boat in a bath. Torn from sullen grey waters, waves were breaking on deck. We were shipping water, not making way, held until the wind might change. The storm doors were locked, keeping all crew below, unless needed on watch on the bridge astern. I watched the close walls around me; this too will pass.

On the fourth day, the winds backed and we had thirty knots on the port quarter, enough to fill the Topsail on the main, and billow the Fore Course. With a good touch on the helm, we made twelve knots in the direction of Cape Horn. Two nights later *Lord Nelson* arrived in the lee of Islas Navarinas, south of the Beagle Channel, and into calmer waters. The crew were exhausted, some of them were injured; but all were relieved and needing rest. We were to anchor in the east of the channel overnight, waiting for the pilot to guide us past the shore-line wrecks and into port.

The channel here is a wide sea. It's the mouth of a funnel between the tail of the Andes to the north (Tierra del Fuego in Argentina) and the old granite-bare hills of the Antarctic plate (the southernmost islands of Chile). Water fills the rift here between the two ancient rock islands of old Gondwanaland; it shudders with deep quakes and Erebus still smoulders. To the west the channel narrows as the mountains steepen. Daily in the afternoons a strong westerly develops, pulling air down the slopes, the Venturi effect building a gale. At night the waters can be calm, deceptive. It was thus on our arrival.

The weather system which spat us out three days south had drawn squalls in its tail. Scattering eastwards, speckled clouds moved over the mapped surface features on the radar screen. With each shower the wind changed and quickened, to disappear as quickly as it had come. "Nellie" rocked on her port anchor, secure, and the worn crew retired to quarters.

Stowing sails in Beagle Channel.

No officer was posted on the watch. We'd left, by then, the unknowable dangers of the ice. Ice bergs moving at night to crush us, carving glaciers to swamp us, growlers to scrape the hull and grind the rudder and props, pack ice to hold us fast. We'd left the Antarctic Ocean with its terrible beauty and fascinating life; crossed over the Convergence, heading north. We'd been ashore on the loneliest outposts, visited by seasonal cruise-ships-full daily in sudden overdoses of human company. The decks had been swept of snow, and ice fell from frozen rigging on the watch on our open bridge. We'd helmed through sunlit frozen gorges, navigating fields of brash-ice, silently singing praises for creation, and finding poetry revealed. We'd sailed past the graveyard of bergs, a cul-de-sac of close islands in a vortex. We'd laughed with penguins, and thrilled together at the spouting, breaching, waving whales. Throughout the cold was untamed, unforgiving, though it was still summer.

All this was behind us, the stormy homeward passage complete, and we eased within reach of port. Ushuaia, with its hotels, bars, humankind and promise of permanent warmth, was the end of the voyage.

Beagle Channel.

Feeling guilty, I volunteered for double anchor watch, midnight to eight. There were two of us to take twenty-minute readings of anchor vectors and read wind speed, to watch the ship and tread the boards quietly around the sleeping crew. The midnight wind was steadily west at 10-15 knots, lapping water gently on our hull, and a shore-light steady from Argentina in the north-west. We chatted idly about home, sailors returning.

Then I saw radar snow bearing densely on us. The wind suddenly grew to 20-25-30 knots…. I called the duty officer from their quarters below. By this time the squall had given us 40 knots, tearing down the funnel between the mountains, the hail thundering on the deckhouse roof. The Bosun arrived, struggling into her heavy weather gear, followed by the Captain. The change of ship's motion had wakened them, as a mother hears the smallest cry.

"Wake the bosun's mates, call an engineer." The Captain was fully roused, alert, standing legs braced against the sudden motion, and staring at the radar.

Lord Nelson bucked and pulled at her chain.

Staccato: "That's not the chain stretching. The anchor's dragging."

Facts: "We're making one knot over the ground; heading for the rocks."

Suddenly the Nav. Room was full of people. Captain issued orders, calmly but positively. I went up to the exposed bridge with the engineer, who was to start both engines. She arrived hurriedly in shorts; I was sent below to gather warm clothes and oilies. We were to weigh anchor under power, and head for safe waters. The BMs roused the port fo'c'sle ready to lay the anchor chain in the locker below. The Bosun and I went far forward to the capstan and chain, to see it lifted cleanly. It was still dark, 4 a.m. with heavy sea and hard rain.

"OK. Start: slow. Stop, STOP!"

"Damn the hydraulics!"

The Capstan drive stopped irregularly, and I'd have to jiggle the handle.

As our anchor cleared the water, we swung round and motored back into the channel. The waiting light in Argentina returned to its position, and by day-break we were re-anchored in a calmer sea. The squall passed. We were wet and cold and safe.

The cook made breakfast early. All the crew were awake, stunned by the suddenness of danger, suddenly averted.

On the white-board in the crew's mess, a plea was scribbled later….

"LOST --------- THREE HOURS SLEEP,
ANYONE SEEN IT?

Please report sightings to Peter"

By mid-afternoon, our arrival in Ushuaia, with its colours, its buildings, people, and ship was uneventful. We were all tired. We'd been living on adrenaline and endless tea for the whole voyage.

We'd sailed our beautiful ship into the ice like Captain Cook. Unlike many an earlier ship, we returned. We marvelled, humbled by the bravery of these men sailing into their dangerous unknown. Some of us crew were bodily disabled, and many had sailed beyond private frontiers. We had all been on the same journey, relying on each other as a team, learning to value and to enhance others' abilities, and our own. Through this, the way ahead is open.

Photo: Marcin Bowbrowolski

Ushuaia to Ushuaia – by Kate Hirst

Susceptibility to seasickness meant I had never considered a trip on *Lord Nelson*. I get hopelessly seasick on anything bigger than a kayak (I even feel queasy playing with bathtub toys). So, when I had a look round *Lord Nelson* in Auckland, here as part of a tall ship festival, I still wasn't thinking of doing a trip. Even the gentle movement of the ship alongside made me feel a bit icky. Then I saw she was going to Antarctica.

Antarctica has been on my bucket list for many years. I had investigated doing a cruise but being a wheelchair user meant that, while the cruise companies could accommodate me on board, they couldn't offer "landings" once we got to Antarctica. I knew that would frustrate me, so I shelved the idea. *Lord Nelson* awoke that dream in me again.

People think I am adventurous. I suspect my brain is underdeveloped in the risk department. I have used a wheelchair since 1990 when I was involved in a gliding accident. The instructor landed us too hard in a muddy field in Leicestershire, broke the glider into matchsticks and I was left paraplegic. I knew straight away that my life had changed forever, but more importantly, I knew I was lucky to be alive. I could feel straight away that I had broken my back and I remember a very strong feeling that I wanted to live, to survive.

That's been the way I have looked at my accident ever since – as a second chance. I have focused on what I have gained, rather than what I have lost. So far, I've gained 25 years. Of course, I have my off-days and know that I have lost out on some things too. But mostly, being injured made me realise that I have to take every opportunity that comes along, do the things I want to do, with the people I want to be with, and be the person I want to be.

Since my accident I have done one or two things that you could say were a bit adventurous, like rafting and kayaking through the Grand Canyon (twice), going on safari in Tanzania, learning to sit-ski (I'm rubbish at it), kayaking in Canada, Alaska, and other parts of the USA and New Zealand, abseiling, parachuting and migrating across the globe. My deciding to sail to Antarctica on a square-rigged tall ship didn't come as much of a surprise to my friends and family.

I managed to get a berth on the trip from a cancellation, which meant I had two months to get organized, get the gear, flights and enough seasickness patches to cover my entire body for three weeks. Arriving onto *Lord Nelson* alongside in Ushuaia was the first time I met my buddy, Sue, and the Watch Leader JC.

The buddy is one of the key volunteer roles on board voyages for those with disabilities. If your disability means that you might need additional support while on board, then you are teamed up with a buddy. You also get a "spacious" cabin to share (whoever wrote that on the website should work in real estate). The buddy is not necessarily experienced in either sailing or supporting a person with a disability. They are simply willing, able, and kind enough to take on the buddy role to support someone with a disability, to get the most out of their voyage. The buddy and buddee are not introduced prior to the voyage. Not surprisingly (to anyone who knows me), having a buddy I got on with was my main concern about the trip (not waves the size of buildings or the horizontal hailstones on night watches – I didn't know about those yet). I am very independent: annoyingly so at times and I was concerned that I'd get buddied with someone who didn't understand and respect this. I needn't have worried. Sue and I hit it off immediately and thanked our lucky stars for this on a daily basis.

The buddy isn't there to be your "carer" but to help with things that might be a bit more challenging because you are on a ship, for example, getting dressed to go up on watch. Like most people, it usually takes me a few minutes to get dressed. On board *Lord Nelson*, getting up for some of the night watches, it could take me 45 minutes. "One hand for the ship" leaving only one hand to pull on underwear (try putting on a bra with one hand), a pair of thermal long johns, a pair of warm trousers, a pair of outer trousers, three pairs of socks, a pair of boots, 5 or 6 upper layers and then the safety harness and balaclava, hat, scarf and two pairs of gloves.

It was easier to do most of this on my bunk, which is a tight enough squeeze.

Sue meanwhile would be pulling on her weezle (a cross between a sleeping bag and onesie) and her own several layers before helping me with the last bits of my dressing (usually pulling my over-trousers up – a challenge at the best of times in a wheelchair, but in rough seas, below-decks in the semi-dark, trying not to disturb our sleeping neighbours, and often sniggering a lot, it became an art form. It mostly consisted of Sue giving me a full wedgie). Add to this being in a heated confined space, and we were often left sweating, laughing and exhausted before we then made the journey from our spacious cabin up the narrow corridor to the lift.

Sue would "spot" me from behind and I would use a loose interpretation of "one hand for the ship" as I ricocheted from one handhold to the next. In fact, down below decks the confined spaces mostly make it easy to find hand holds. The difficult areas were getting from one side of the ship to the other to reach the different lifts. Conditions meant that various doors were locked off, so this could mean crossing the ship

Kate and her buddy Sue keeping warm on the bowsprit.

several times to get from bed to watch, and this could take another ten minutes. Each time I crossed the ship from port to starboard or vice versa, Sue would act like a goal-keeper!

On occasion Sue would ask me how she could help and I couldn't answer. Feeling pathetic, exhausted, cold and with a lack of experience in this environment; all I could say was "I don't know". Not much help to her! Sue is amazing though; she managed to balance supporting me just the right amount, while not being overprotective or patronising. And at times, the jobs were no fun. When seasickness and a stomach bug were going round the ship, everyone literally "mucked in" to dispose of sick bags and I was glad to be able to repay some of her kindness. And you certainly bond over those things. "Thank goodness I got you!" became our ritual mantra.

We were also lucky to have a great bunch of people on our watch who have also become friends. I have great memories of the scenery, the sheer number of different shades of white and blue and textures in each ice berg, the smell of penguin poo, glaciers cracking and popping, the sound of a pod of hump back whales breathing as they slowly made their way past the ship not 20m away, but what keeps the memories alive is sharing them, having shared them. On a voyage you get to share day to day life with a group of 50 strangers, hauling on ropes, being on lookout, learning how to helm, learning about sailing, but also playing Uno, doing happy hour together, mess duty, nights in the bar, night watches, day watches, laughing, huddled up together to shelter from the weather, hot drinks on a cold night, decorating birthday cakes (Sue's great at making penguins from icing).

Penguin birthday cake for Kate.

On a voyage like that, you get to know people in a particular way. It's in a narrow context but it is deep and intense, as by turns you suffer and enjoy real extremes. Sue and I were so lucky to get paired up, and we have remained friends since. When I returned to England on Leg 10 sailing into London, Sue came to see *Lord Nelson* in and presented me with the most beautifully hand-decorated cake with penguins all over the top. She had been practising!

Dates		Distances in Nautical Miles				Maximum Wind Force
Start	End	Total	Under Sail	Motor-Sailing	Motoring	
16.02.14	12.03.14	1997	110	1209	678	10

Photo: Skip Novak

Leg 7

Ushuaia to Punta del Este by Captain Barbara Campbell

13th March – The crew joined on time and training commenced straight after introductions. In the evening many crew went ashore to post cards, wander around Ushuaia and have a drink. I filled out our application for a permit to go to the Falkland Islands. As this permit takes 5 to 7 working days and is free I could not understand why it had not been applied for earlier, as it would have given us the option. Our next port had to be either Puerto Madryn in Argentina, or the Falkland Islands, as we had not taken enough fuel or victuals for

the passage to Buenos Aires, given the inflated prices in Ushuaia.

At the port's request, we had an early departure on 14th. The 15 to 20 knot wind on the beam pinned us on the berth; fortunately we had an anchor out. Slowly we pulled ourselves off the berth before turning round and proceeding eastwards down Beagle Channel. Hail, rain and sleet all contrived to make it a cold and somewhat damp transit. The temperature reached a maximum of

Crew having a crab dinner at Freddies Restaurant, Ushuaia.

It reads: Prohibited mooring for English pirate ships!

5 degrees in the afternoon. All on board wished to go round Cape Horn, but the wind, a steady SW'ly 25 knots, was not due to decrease until after midnight. I decided to reduce speed to 3 knots as soon as the pilot disembarked at 1800. This would allow the strongest winds to pass, before we entered the open seas and headed for Cape Horn.

overhead. Snow covered the high ground whilst low cloud hung around until mid-afternoon. We passed three miles south of Cape Horn heading west, before turning round, bracing the yards, and setting Topsails. We sailed and drifted east back past Cape Horn, handing sail before dinner. In the evening Fred the Fish caught a tuna. I could not get over the fact that Cape Horn is 56 degrees South and is so different from where I live on the Clyde Estuary, at 56 degrees North.

OK, you have the biggest flag!

Aft port on watch, have they spotted Cape Horn?

Midnight to 0700 saw the last of the strong SW winds go through and by 0900 the wind had eased to 10 knots. As we motored towards Cape Horn, the sea unbelievably became flat calm. It is rare that the seas at Cape Horn are quiet and not every day that one can have "afternoon tea off Cape Horn". We enjoyed both tea and calm as albatrosses wheeled and played

The tide was not favourable in the Le Maire Straits until 1220 16th, so we proceeded slowly northwards. The gaskets were loosed on the Fore T'Gallant, Topsails and Courses. Following a Sunday Service at 1100, we set sails. The winds increased to 15 knots from the NW and all square sails bar the Main Royal were set. At 1130 we were only making 4 knots but this increased

BM off Cape Horn.

Photo: David Mercer

with the flood tide and at 1600 we touched 10 knots. Once clear of the Le Maire Straits we sailed in a NE direction in 15 to 20 knots of NW wind.

As we were still unsure as to our next port, to keep options open we continued NE towards the middle of the Falkland Islands. In the early hours the wind fell light, but the following morning we were making a steady 5 knots under sail. By afternoon I had to make a decision and decided we would bear away towards Port Stanley and the east side of the Falkland Islands. Luckily we got an email from Andy Spark, Ship Operations Manager, saying we were to proceed to Port Stanley and not Puerto Madryn. Puerto Madryn turned out to

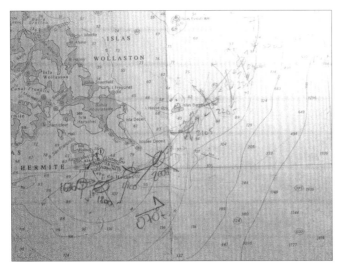

The chart showing the route from Cape Horn.

be another extortionately priced Argentinian port with a US$ 20,000 price tag for the pilots and berth. We were all delighted with this news. In the evening the wind shifted to the SSW and, with the watch, BMs, and a few stragglers, we braced the yards and set the Outer Jib.

18th March – In the SSW'ly force 6 wind we averaged 8 knots overnight. As we approached the South Coast of the Falkland Islands, Commerson's Penguins surprised us with a visit, happily playing alongside. Another email from Andy Spark said that we could go to the Military base at Mare Harbour for fuel. As we were in danger of sailing past Mare Harbour before confirmation came through, we clewed up the Fore Course to slow down and braced the yards. Just before 1500, Mare Harbour was confirmed; all hands were called and at 1600 we started engines and handed sail in time for the 1700 QHM Pilot, Chris Locke, a really nice guy who gave us plenty of information. A big Dutch tug with a 65 tonne bollard pull accompanied us in! The

Pilot boat approaching the ship on the way into Mare Harbour, Falklands.

tug was not so useful when we were coming alongside but was brilliant at plucking us off the berth so that big yokohama fenders could be re-positioned. We had no passes for the military base, so the crew had to spend the evening on board.

I decided to spend two nights alongside, enabling the crew to walk the 4-hour round trip to Bertha's Beach and see the Gentoo penguins. Bertha's beach is one of the best wildlife sites in the Falkland Islands with a Gentoo penguin rookery, terns and Commerson's dolphins playing in the surf. All the crew went off with packed lunches. The rookery was behind the beach and the crew were asked to stay close to the beach, approach the penguins slowly and sit down and let the penguins come to them. There were only about 20 penguins but the crew enjoyed seeing them and it was a bracing walk. Bunker fuel was taken by the ship in the morning. Everyone at the Base was very helpful and we had Open Ship for the Military and their families in the afternoon. Two thousand people live on the base, similar to the population of Port Stanley. In the evening the crew had passes for the military base and went there in buses. They bought wifi cards, went bowling, enjoyed a few drinks in the mess, did a little shopping or had a coffee. I checked with Andy and the permit had not come through for our permission to call into the Falklands, and it never did. Our visit to the Falklands made it doubtful that we would subsequently call into an Argentinian port.

Magellanic and Gentoo penguins on Bertha's Beach.
Photo: David Mercer

Penguin rookery behind Bertha's Beach.

As we had nine VC places spare for the sail to Port Stanley on 20th, I offered them to those who had helped us. The extras for the day sail were the pilot, a young officer from *HMS Clyde*, plus two others. We used the aft spring to get off the berth. The 35 knot wind was from ahead and we crawled out of the harbour at 3 to 4 knots. As we did so, the pilot told me he had that moment officially shut the harbour as it was too windy! He could not shut it earlier as he wanted to sail with us!

Sails were set in time for morning smoko and we soon made 7 knots. The 40 mile sail to Port Stanley was brilliant, with strong winds and low seas; our extra crew joined in with gusto. At 1500 we handed sail, started engines and proceeded towards Port William and through the narrows to Port Stanley. We moored alongside East Jetty (the Falkland Island Company kindly let us use it free of charge), and were all fast for 1730. At 1800 I called the crew together to inform them that our final port would be in Uruguay and not Buenos Aires, Argentina. I explained the reasons and the huge cost of going to Buenos Aires. The pilot fees alone were US$19,000 one-way and the pilotage and berth fees would come to a staggering US$45,000 each turnaround. Most of the crew understood the reasoning and I told them the JST would pay for them to get to Buenos Aires from Uruguay for their flight home. The crew were free to go ashore and the following afternoon we organised a popular half day tour round the battlefield sites. The tour stopped at a village hall for coffee and chat with locals. The Governor and local TV came down to the ship for a tour and photos.

Wreck of a sailing ship near Port Stanley where the SAS hid from the Argentinians behind the lines in 1982.
Photo: David Mercer

Monument dedicated to the memory of the men of the Fleet Auxiliary Service who lost their lives at Fitzroy 08/06/82 in defence of the Falklands.

Before giving the good folk of Port Stanley a great sight, we opened ship again to the public. We then sailed off the berth, even though we were facing in the opposite direction to the entrance. Prior to letting go our stern spring the Fore Topsail was set aback. The after watches then braced the fore yards round as we turned off the berth. The main Topsail and Outer Jib were set as we sailed eastwards in Stanley Harbour. Then it was hands to bracing stations to brace to starboard for sailing through the narrows. Once into Port William we again squared the yards for the five-mile transit to the open sea. The VC were kept on their toes. Whilst the Fore Course was being set it caught on a forestay split pin, resulting in an 8" tear. Knowing we would need the sail, I went aloft straight away and carried out a herringbone repair. Late afternoon we set the sail and were soon making 8 knots in 30 to 35 knots of W'ly wind. This was a great wind direction for us and I knew we had to make the most of it because the forecasts showed the winds becoming NW'ly by Tuesday.

Overnight we had frequent gusts to 40 knots. The wind did not let up at all and remained SW 25 to 30 knots, gusting 40 knots all day. The combined seas and swell were about 6 metres. We averaged about 6 knots, in a NNW direction. This was a great sail but very trying for everyone, with big seas and the ship suddenly lurching when we were 'slapped' by a wave or fell into

a trough. Moving around the ship was difficult, and we had extra safety lines and the sailor strainers rigged. The wind gradually dropped to 20 knots and the seas to 2 metres, so we set the T'Gallants and Outer Jib. The sun came out and everyone felt much better after a good night's sleep. In the afternoon the wind picked up to 25 knots so we furled the Main T'Gallant.

Just after midnight on 25th we crossed the latitude of 46 degrees South, 10 degrees north of Cape Horn. The temperature had increased from 4 degrees at Cape Horn to 13 degrees. The night sky was really clear with the Milky Way, Mars and Jupiter as clear as they could possibly get. We continued making 6 knots in a NNE direction. The sun was sparkling and conditions ideal for sailing. The ship felt well balanced, enabling good steady helming.

On 26th I gave a talk to the crew on Celestial Navigation, including everyone using a sextant. The noon latitude was only 1.2 miles different to the GPS! The PC had an enclosed space rescue drill. Fred the Fish caught a tuna and Colin made another great birthday cake, this time for Marco. I spoke with the crew and informed them that Punta del Este in Uruguay had been confirmed as our turnaround port.

Synchronised swimming.

Distinctive Southern Right Dolphin Whales played alongside the ship on the 27th. We were making 8 to 9 knots under sail and though it was great sailing, the N'ly wind meant that we were making a course of 080 degrees. Sadly, at 1700, we handed sail and started the engines. This was the first time we had used them since our arrival in Port Stanley and sail power alone had driven us for over five days. This was to be our best day for catching tuna, with a total of nine small ones for the day. Sushi for lunch again!

The sea temperature reached 20 degrees. This was checked several times but proved to be true. The day was overcast with prolonged periods of rain. We heard from Andy Spark that we could anchor off Piriapolis. This was good news, and the crew were pleased to hear we would call in somewhere before Punta del Este. Sperm whales paid us a visit; perhaps they were after the tuna too as we caught eight today. Sushi for lunch and dinner, but it was never boring, with arborio rice a good substitute for sushi rice!

Jenny and her handmade Uruguayan flag.

The 29th was a lovely sunny day, and after happy hour we had a number of dedicated sunbathers on deck. For the BMs there were a few aloft jobs that needed doing, now that the seas had calmed down. For the Captain there was a blown seam of 30cm on the Fore Topsail, that had to be done before the sail could be re-set. Late afternoon we braced the yards to port as the wind was due to become NNE by morning, and we were all hopeful we would be sailing again the next day. In the evening Vicki, MP, ran an entertaining quiz. Once again we had a clear sky at night; Mars, Venus, Scorpio, and my favourite, Zubenelgenubi, all visible.

By dawn the wind was NNE 25 knots and we were making only 4 knots under engines. After the morning meeting we set Topsails, Courses and Fore T'Gallants and bore away, soon making 6 knots and a course 25 degrees off the course required. I figured it would be better than motoring at 4 knots in the correct direction. There was a short Sunday Service on a windswept deck. The wind remained 25 knots all day, giving us an exhilarating sail. At 1930 we clewed up sail and started engines to head towards Piriapolis under fore and aft sail. At 2345 there was a sudden wind-shift and the wind increased to 30 knots. We called out the BMs and with two watches braced the yards and set the Main Staysail. In the shallow waters of the Rio Plata, we rolled and rolled, so there was little sleep for anyone.

The following day the wind had decreased to 20 knots so we set Topsails, stopped engines and sailed across the dark brown waters of the Rio Plata. After lunch we called all crew to hand sail and anchored 0.35 mile off the breakwater at Piriapolis. The agent turned up at 1600 and I went with him ashore by launch, to clear immigration. We rolled gently at anchor but the crew enjoyed a good BBQ. Everyone was tired so most crew were turned in by 2200. It was gone midnight before the agent finally brought the passports back, together with the clearance papers.

At 0930 the following morning we started running the VC ashore. They really enjoyed the laid-back holiday town of Piriapolis. Many crew took the cable car up a nearby hill. The more energetic walked on the sandy

VC and BM's enjoying the ride in the doti boat.

smoothly and after lunch the crew were free to go ashore.

There was free time the following morning followed by open ship in the afternoon and a last night meal in the evening. The flight and ferry tickets were bought for the crew to get to Buenos Aires.

On 5th we had a big happy hour followed by open ship to the public for two hours. About ten VC left the ship as they wanted the extra time in Buenos Aires. The remaining VC left at 0445 or at 0630 on the 6th, depending on whether they were getting the flight or the ferry.

This had been a brilliant trip which covered a vast range of sights: from Ushuaia, through the Beagle Channel to Cape Horn, then onwards to the Falkland Islands and north to the warmer weather in Uruguay. Albatrosses, whales and other wildlife abounded and graced us with their presence. The only blot was the change from Buenos Aires to Uruguay, which disappointed many. However we put in great efforts to make it as painless as possible for the crew to get back to Buenos Aires. All the transport, right from the taxi at the ship to arrival in Buenos Aires, was organised.

The sailing was outstanding, with 60% of the total distance being under sail. As to the VC, the voyage surpassed their expectations.

beaches or further inland, and a few had a swim. A sea-lion sunned itself close to where we landed the crew in the marina. It was clearly a pet sea-lion and it delighted the crew and provided excellent photo opportunities. The Permanent Crew and BMs did some rig work and sent down the Outer Jib for repair before having a half day. By 1900 all the crew were back onboard and by 2200 the bar was quiet.

We sailed off the anchor again, without even starting engines, and sailed in a S'ly direction. However we could not continue making this course as Punta del Este lay to the ENE. At 1330 we clewed up sail for the last time this voyage. The wind picked up to 20 knots and we had a 'bash' to windward. We anchored to the east of Gorriti Island at 1830, just 0.5 miles from Punta Del Este Breakwater. After dinner we had the Egg Drop and then a night in the bar during which the Ensign and Chart were auctioned.

On the 3rd, the 2nd Mate and I went into the port to check the berth out whilst the crew harbour-stowed the sails. We weighed anchor and I turned the ship outside the port, reversing to our berth. The berth was well made and the marina new. We got alongside

Dates		Distances in Nautical Miles				Maximum Wind Force
Start	End	Total	Under Sail	Motor-Sailing	Motoring	
13.03.14	06.04.14	1963	1172	523	268	8

Ushuaia to Punta del Este – by Fred Normandale

Anyone with any interest in sailing ships and the days of sail must want to see Cape Horn. I most certainly did, so when the opportunity arose to join 'Nelly' in Ushuaia on a leg of her Round the World voyage, I jumped at the chance.

Along with my pal, Colin the Baker and brother-in-law Dave Mercer, I flew to Buenos Aires then south to Ushuaia. It was autumn, raining and about 2 degrees above zero with snow on the mountains beyond the town when we arrived. *Lord Nelson* was alongside and just back from her epic voyage to the Antarctic under Captain Chris Phillips, having encountered an exceedingly stormy northerly crossing of the Drake Passage on her return.

Ushuaia.

When she sailed again, now with Captain Barbara Campbell in command, adverse winds, though reasonable weather, meant we motored to a position three miles due south of the island that is Cape Horn. Just west of Cape Horn we about turned and set sail. I'd seen the awesome, grim, austere southernmost tip of South America where so many ships had come to grief while attempting to reach the west coast of the great continent. This sighting, for me, was a lifetime ambition fulfilled.

Initially the programme said we were to sail along the Argentinian coast, calling in at various ports and ending in Buenos Aires. Sadly the exorbitant charges in Ushuaia for harbour dues and piloting and the expectation of more of the same made this plan cost prohibitive. It was time for Plan B. Captain Barbara charted a course for the Falkland Islands. What a bonus! This would be another tick in the 'book of life' experiences.

When all the sails were set and we were making good speed I put a speculative fishing line over the stern, not expecting anything, but trying. Within ten minutes a big fish took the lure. This specimen took some hauling in, and was just in photo range from cameras on the bridge when it dropped off the hook, causing strong language from me and several 'the one that got away' comments from the watch on lookout.

Marco and David Mercer.
This is bigger than anything Fred caught.

With the line back out, twenty minutes later it was 'fish on' again. This time a smaller (of course) big-eyed tuna took the lure and was landed on the stern platform. This fish was big enough to feed the entire crew, but sadly the fishing activity attracted many large seabirds including albatross and I was compelled to take the line in.

The birds continued to follow the ship and it was several days later before it occurred to me that a small, wooden paravane with lure extended behind, would dive below the surface, keeping the hook out of the reach of the birds. Dave and I made a device from a bit of wood and almost immediately began catching fish again. Albacore tuna made great sushi starters and superb dinners.

It was a sail-cracking passage to the Falklands, where we received a great reception from the locals, spending two nights berthed at the Mount Pleasant Military Base followed by two nights alongside in Stanley.

Captain Barbara had been ashore on the first day and said she had walked about four miles along the coastline to a 'rookery'. "We're in the Falklands," I thought. "Who wants to see rooks? And what's more, I haven't seen any trees." How was I to know penguins lived in a rookery?

Gentoo and Magellinic Penguins, Bertha's Beach.

Derek the Cook had a strange experience while shopping for provisions in Stanley. Among other items, he bought potatoes, which, when he checked the bill, realized they cost a fortune because they were imported. He returned half of them. Potatoes were on ration.

Falkland Island Kelp Goose.

Cookie also ordered lots of joints of local mutton, which arrived in the form of three whole carcasses, to be dismembered. These were quickly strung up in the little galley, then hacksaws from the engineers and an axe were utilised by Derek, with helpful assistance from Caroline, the Aussie doctor: usually a gynecologist!

All hands toured the 'battlefields', which the locals took great pleasure in conducting, and at no charge. Donations were requested and supplied for the upkeep of the local Community Centre. This was a very moving tour for everyone, and for some a tearful experience.

My impression of the Falklands in autumn was of desolate, windswept, treeless islands, though with extremely friendly, patriotic inhabitants. 'Sailing' off the berth with many islanders watching from various

Bluff Cove where on the disastrous day 08/06/82 the troopships Sir Galahad and Sir Tristram were attacked as they were landing men.

vantage points around the bay was an impressive, memorable departure. It was special to be a part of the enthusiastic waving and horn sounding that took place between the ship and the spectators.

Typical Falkland flora.

Photo: David Mercer

Captain Barbara announced that, having been to the Falkland Islands, we would no longer be welcome in Argentina. Instead, a course was set for the north bank of the River Plate and for Uruguay. Another bonus! This was also a country I never thought I'd visit.

The weather grew warmer as we progressed north and west and shorts were broken out by most. We continued enjoying favourable winds, sailed well and still caught fish. This was now a welcome alternative, in many guises, to the constant mutton and the cook's versatile ways of preparing it. Fishing ceased again for a while, a couple days out of the River Plate when a big, black triangular fin was seen in the wake of the ship and both lures and 110lb breaking strain line were snatched, parting like cotton.

Arriving in Uruguay we anchored off at Piriapolis, a small resort town, and took the VC ashore in the Doti boat to explore what was a very cultured and civilized country. The Spanish-speaking natives were extremely welcoming and friendly. A chairlift took many of the crew to the top of a big hill overlooking the bay, from where Nelly looked like a pinhead.

At anchor off Piriapolis, River Plate.

Photo: David Mercer

We stayed at anchor overnight then sailed further up the mighty river to Punta Del Este and the end of our fantastic voyage.

It wasn't a simple flight home to the UK from Uruguay. We were bussed to Montevideo then took a very short plane trip across the River Plate to Buenos Aires to catch our return flight across the Atlantic. I looked hard from the window of the little plane but there was no view of the wreck of the *Graf Spee*.

On our arrival in Argentina we were instructed by the ship's agent to say we'd been on a cruise holiday, ending in Uruguay, rather than sailing on the *Lord Nelson*. This clearly worked though the immigration officers were not happy to see 'Falklands Islands' stamped in our passports (I was!).

What a fabulous voyage this had been. It had indeed been the trip of a lifetime (and there was still fish in the freezer for the next leg of Nellie's epic circumnavigation!).

The collage Fred made up from some of his favourite photos from the voyage. The GPS position is Cape Horn.

Ushuaia to Punta del Este by Murray Carmichael

It was high summer in Argentina, temperature of 24°C, and the sun blazing out of an azure blue sky. I felt totally out of place in the bus while changing airports in Buenos Aires, dressed in heavy sailing gear and boots, while everyone else wore T-shirts and shorts. The internal flight South to Tierra del Fuego flew over the arid landscape of Patagonia with the snow-peaked Chilean Andes off to starboard. It was only after descending through cloud to land at Ushuaia, at 54° 48´S, the world's most southerly city, and seeing other passengers donning woolly hats and thick jackets that I realised that even summer here was cold. We emerged to heavy rain and sleet, reminiscent of Edinburgh in January.

After signing on as "Voyage Crew" we were introduced to the PC: Captain Barbara Campbell, First and Second Mates, Bosun, Engineers, Nurse/Purser and Cook, all qualified professionals. Four experienced Bosun's Mates and a Cook's Assistant, all unpaid but enjoying a free passage, looked after 35 paying volunteers allocated to four watches. There were no disabled people on this trip but most of us were over 65 and having a "skiing" holiday (spending kids' inheritance), doing the things of which we had long dreamt while there was still time. On my previous JST voyages, there were crew members in wheelchairs, amputees on crutches, deaf and blind, all taking a full part in sailing the ship. Blind helmsmen, using the speaking compass, can keep better courses than most sighted volunteers. Lifts, disabled toilets and showers are provided and anchor points around the ship allow the wheelchair users to be independent and take part in watch duties. Often their upper body strength is an asset when heaving down on halyards. Hand rails with braille markings give blind crew assistance in moving about the ship.

On mess duty making sushi from the many tuna caught.

I was given my watch card showing the 24 hour duties allocated to the "Forward Starboard" watch for the next ten days. Divided into seven duty periods, in correct naval style, the times advance each day to give everyone an equal share of day and night watches. Once a week we are allocated to mess duties, which involves assisting in the kitchen and serving in the mess. Each of the four watches, when on duty, provides the helmsman (no auto-helm allowed) and lookouts. We keep an hourly log of weather, course, speed and sea state and report to the duty deck officer. Sail changes are carried out by the duty watch, assisted by the rest of the crew when required. Everyone is required to take part in "happy hour" which involves cleaning the ship, polishing the brass and scrubbing the decks.

Beagle Channel.

Before departure the volunteers were given a briefing by the officers and then an introduction to the ship, showing where the different ropes are situated and how to operate them. *Lord Nelson* is a barque with square-rigged fore and main masts, each carrying a Course (main), Topsail, T'Gallant and Royal sail. The yards have to be braced depending on the wind angle and the sails furled as required. All this is done manually by teams, lining the deck, hauling on heavy bracing lines and halyards. Stowing the sails requires crew to climb the rigging and out along the yards. The various bracing, bunt and clewlines, halyards and sheets are made from plain hemp of differing diameter, but no fancy colours as seen on yachts. There is a "pin diagram" of the 40 belaying points on each rail and a further 30 around the masts. Having some twenty to thirty inexperienced sailors setting sails or bracing the yards, which involves pulling or letting off several ropes in unison, can be a time consuming exercise

Friday 14th – Stores loaded, practice mast climbs complete, we were preparing to cast off when a naval band struck up on the quayside. This was not for us, but to welcome the arrival of a Chilean navy training sailing ship. We slipped, unnoticed, past the large sign declaring the Malvinas to be Argentinian, and up the Beagle Channel bound for Cape Horn. The disdain showed by the Argentinian navy to our ensign may hark back to 26th April 1982 when their cruiser, the

Untying gaskets.

General Belgrano, departed from this dock for its fatal rendezvous with *HMS Conqueror* six days later. We followed in the path of Captain Fitzroy and his young ornithologist Charles Darwin in 1831. Three cooked meals a day, with mid-morning "Smoko" of coffee and home baking, and afternoon tea and biscuits kept us all over-nourished. Terns, fulmars, petrels and albatrosses wheeled above our wake, while dolphins and occasional whales splashed alongside. Our 2000 to midnight watch, out on the open bridge, was very cold, with the odd hail shower to ward off drowsiness and keep the lookouts alert.

Southern Ocean.

Saturday 15th – The following day the wind died and we motored out to Cape Horn. Not for us the legendary, crashing seas and spume-laden air, but a great black rock on a placid sea. Kape Hoorn Island, named by the Dutch explorer, Willem Shouten, in 1616, in honour of his birth place, Hoorn, is Chilean territory and we received radio messages from their authorities requesting our identity and intended course. Photos taken, we turned around and headed north.

Murray at Cape Horn.

Sunday 16th – During our midnight to 0400 watch the clouds cleared and we witnessed the amazing panoply of Southern stars, with the Southern Cross nesting amongst the dense mass of stars in the "Milky Way". As the moon rose the sails took on luminescence, like a scene from the "Pirates of the Caribbean". As we headed north the wind strengthened, more sail was set, and engines stopped, as we took advantage of a 4 knot tidal current between the mainland and Staten Island.

Monday 17th – On the following day the wind got up and "Nellie", as she is familiarly known, took off with spray and waves washing down her decks. The following seas made her difficult to hold on a steady course, and several caustic messages about our helming abilities were relayed from the Captain. It was St Patrick's Day and after our last watch we repaired to the bar to enjoy a glass of Guinness or two. However, Captain Barbara had other ideas and we were summoned on deck to hand the Course sail. After a fairly bumpy night those who had not had the foresight to take their anti-seasickness pills were suffering badly. It did mean that there were "seconds" of bacon and eggs for the rest of us.

Murray and watch at Cape Horn.

Tuesday 18th – The Falkland Islands came into view. Our first stop was to the naval base at Port Mare where we were met by the Queen's Harbour Master, Chris, who came out to meet us on a large Dutch tug and piloted us in, to tie up in front of *HMS Clyde*, the River Class patrol vessel defending our territorial waters. On the following day we had a "run ashore" to visit Bertha's beach, where we watched a group of Magellanic and Gentoo penguins doing their silly walk up the beach, while dolphins swam in the surf looking out for any tasty fledglings brave enough to go swimming. On the bare hillside and in the skies were a profusion of upland and ruddy headed geese, cormorants, gulls, skuas and the striated caracara, the "Johnny Rook" of the Falkland Islands, which feed on dead penguins. A visit to the River Class patrol boat, *HMS Clyde*, just before she departed with a company of Marines for an exercise on Antarctica, was arranged. The evening excursion was to the Mount Pleasant military base where we enjoyed

cheap beer in the NAAFI and played 10-pin bowling with the squaddies. The wind freshened overnight and, during our 0200-0400 harbour watch, we paid keen attention to the warps, which had been doubled in anticipation.

Aboard *HMS Clyde*.

Thursday 20th – Early next morning, with the QHM, Chris aboard plus a few well wishers, we left for Port Stanley. Chris's last duty act was to close Port Mare to all traffic, because the wind speed was over the set limit, before steering us out to the open sea. With a force 7 wind behind us we made a fast, but fairly bumpy passage to Port Stanley and tied up alongside a rather ramshackle jetty. It was the cook's night off so we repaired to a local hotel for an excellent supper of local goose pâté and lamb.

Port Stanley looks just as it did in the 1980s news pictures, with its brightly coloured houses, its cathedral, the governor's house and the memorials to battles and shipwrecks from two world wars and the Argentinian conflict. We took a minibus tour into the interior, across the barren landscape where rivers of boulders, brought down in the last Ice Age, intersect acres of scrubland partially closed off by fences bearing

Bertha's Beach.

"Danger Minefield" signs. At the hamlet of Fitzroy we saw memorials to the men killed and wounded on the disastrous day of 8th June 1982, when the troopships *Sir Galahad* and *Sir Tristram* were attacked by Argentinian jets as they were landing men on Bluff Cove. Returning to Stanley we viewed Mounts Harriet and Tumbledown, captured, after fierce fighting, by 3 Commando Brigade and the Scots Guards, who finished the battle with a bayonet charge. We had two Argentinian crew members aboard and it was interesting to hear their views on the conflict.

Saturday 22nd March – With many Islanders watching from the shore we sailed off our berth. The Fore Topsail was set aback to blow the bow off the quay, before lines were let go aft. Once turned off the quay, we squared the fore yards, quickly set the Main Topsail and then braced the yards to starboard, before sailing through the narrows at the entrance to the harbour and down William Sound into the open sea. A grand sight for the locals, but the Fore Course sail caught whilst being set, and suffered an 8-inch tear. The Captain then climbed aloft and repaired it with needle and thread. With 20-30 knots of NW wind and yards braced hard to port, we set Main Course, both Topsails, Fore T'Gallant, Inner Jib and Mizzen-Main stay sails. This allowed us to maintain an ENE heading with 10 knots of speed. The list to starboard put the lee portholes under water and made the use of lee cloths mandatory in all berths. The Bosun's Mate, Fred and Dave, laid fishing lines off the stern and were soon pulling in tuna fish, turning the stern platform into a charnel house of blood and fish guts. The very fresh fish made wonderful Sushi for the crew, and the remains fed the scores of albatrosses and petrels wheeling above our stern. On one occasion a large, black, dorsal finned sea creature, thought to be a shark, took both lines with attached fish in a single gulp!

As we reached lower latitudes the sun became warmer. Shorts and T-shirts came out and even the occasional wave breaking over the deck felt warm. Under instruction by the Captain, we were able to take Meridian Altitude sun sights on the sextant and plot our position on the chart. It was within 3 miles of the GPS. Night watches in the balmy air under a canopy of stars, watching for shooting stars, were a joy.

Sunday 30th March – After a peaceful day at sea, Sunday night proved to be busy. The Captain gave the Cook's Assistant the afternoon off and donned

Government House, Port Stanley.

Monument to the 1982 conflict, Port Stanley.

Falkland terrain.

an apron herself. Post-dinner entertainment came in two parts. First we handed all the square sails, which meant everybody on the foredeck had several saltwater showers. The waves were splashing up from all directions, so both forward watches were equally soaked. Once everybody had changed into dry clothes we gathered in the bar for a talk by Bosun's Mate Fred Normandale, about his childhood growing up in the fishing port of Scarborough, and tales of people he'd known there. He had us enthralled as he described his first trip on a herring drifter at the age of ten, when he'd been terribly seasick. "You think this is bad?" he said as everybody in the bar clutched their drinks in one hand and held on with the other to counteract another of Nellie's huge lurches. "The drifters were bad enough when underway but when we stopped and turned the engines off they positively wallowed."

Our evening watch was exhilarating, with the wind gusting to above 30 knots and a confused sea producing irregular huge swells. Stars came and went as Cumulo-Stratus clouds gathered and dispersed, and with no moon it was a very dark and wild night. Although the motion made it difficult to balance at the wheel, it was probably far more uncomfortable for those trying to sleep below. We were no longer alone in an empty ocean; a ship passed ahead of us, starboard light clearly visible, and two more were identified on the radar. The Captain appeared on deck in the last 15 minutes of our watch and announced that we needed to square the yards and set the main staysail, so the combined forces of Aft Port and Forward Starboard did some midnight sweating and tailing.

Monday 31ˢᵗ – When Monday dawned the sea had moderated a little and Uruguay was in sight off the starboard bow. Several ships were visible in the distance on the port side, and as we got closer we could see that they were anchored cargo vessels. We counted at least 22, which is more than the total number of ships we had seen between leaving Ushuaia and arriving here. Post-breakfast exercise was provided for all hands when we braced the yards and set the Fore Topsail.

Down below several days' worth of furious sewing activity was underway as Jenny, a member of Aft Starboard watch, put the finishing touches to a handcrafted Uruguayan flag. Fortunately it was ready to be hoisted by noon and we were able to make our approach to our anchorage in Piriapolis with the correct courtesy flag flying. We anchored, rocking gently in the swell, looking forward to an evening BBQ and the opportunity to explore Piriapolis the next day. It was a perfect, calm evening with a cloudless sky and, as the sun dipped below the horizon, we saw it. It is not mythical, we all agreed that it happened. The final rays gave off a GREEN FLASH!

Tuesday 1ˢᵗ April – Next day we were ferried ashore by RIB to the harbour, where the slipway was guarded by an enormous sea lion, only grudgingly giving way to us at the last moment and circling the RIB, snorting in derision. After a day of tourism and indulging in Internet access, we returned to the ship and harbour

Jenny proudly hoisting her hand made Uruguayan flag.

night watch. This involves monitoring our position on the radar screen, checking anchor chains and exchanging pleasantries with passing fishermen drawn to us by our floodlit masts.

More fresh fish!

Taking sights.

Wednesday 2nd – We then headed north to Punta Del Este, (34° 58'S, 54° 57' W) our final destination, for a short sail, before anchoring offshore and carrying out a harbour stow of the sails. To achieve the perfect stow involves the crew going aloft and out on the yards. The sails are pulled up on the Buntlines and Clewlines, folded neatly and lifted on top of the yard before being made fast with short lengths of rope called Gaskets. Getting the clew end tucked away is the trickiest part, requiring two people and much tugging, pulling and swearing. That evening the traditional egg drop was held. Each watch is given a raw egg and a competition is held to see who can throw it from the Fore Top platform along the length of the ship without it breaking. Great ingenuity is displayed into padding the egg and working out a line, avoiding the various bits of rigging in the projected flight path. As usual the heavily padded

Bull sea lion guarding the slipway.

rockets, hurled with gusto, revealed their contents truly scrambled and the only egg to survive had been dropped gently in a "hanky" parachute. The winner was rewarded by having his egg broken over his head, by the Captain.

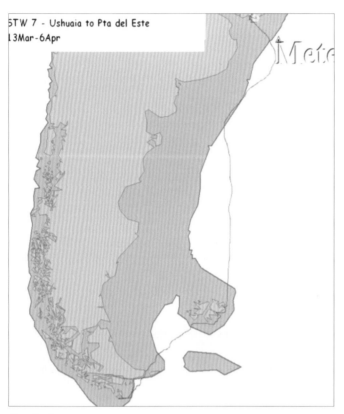

Track chart.

Thursday 3rd – The Captain recklessly allowed me to helm into the narrow harbour, with the First Engineer on the throttles, while she directed us onto a berth near the British, sea-going tug *Astoria*. This luxuriously fitted out and maintained vessel is chartered out during the summer for cruises to Antarctica. The port, on the mouth of the river Plate, is close to the site of the WW2 naval engagement with the German Pocket Battleship the *Admiral Graf Spee* in 1939, and the anchor of *HMS Ajax* is preserved on the foreshore. Although the sea was cold the beaches were warm, the bodies bronzed and the swim attire brief. Cafes and bars stay open late in Uruguay and we had visitors coming out to see the ship until after 1am. They all asked if we knew of their great hero, Louis Suarez, little knowing the disaster that was to follow at the World cup!

Saturday 5th – From here we travelled to Montevideo by bus and crossed the river to Buenos Aries in a superfast ferry, with 1000 passenger capacity, slipping smoothly over the water at 30 knots.

Pre egg drop briefing in the cabin.

Winner of the egg drop.

Piriapolis seafront.

Ushuaia to Punta del Este by Katherine Morris – Cook's Assistant

18/3/14 – When we docked at Mare Harbour (attached to Mount Pleasant Military Base, Falklands), it was exciting to hear British accents so far south! Most of us then visited the base the next evening, went to the 'Gull and Penguin' bar and had a very British night out with too many beers and take away chips.

31/3/14 – Stunning sunset, saw the green flash! It's real!

Ushuaia to Punta del Este by Jorge A San Martino

March 18th – The previous night, I had gone to bed early, at 9 pm; however, it was hard to go to sleep. I was sleeping in the upper berth, which is narrower than the lower one; other crew members walked by, chatted or turned on lights. *Lord Nelson* heaved, pitched, yawed, and rolled by effect of the waves. Everything conspired to make slumber a vain hope. I could hardly get any sleep before midnight, so I woke up just as I'd gone to bed.

The night was freezing cold, so much so that in spite of wearing long underwear, two pairs of trousers, socks

and boots, my legs felt numb. It rained on and off, and even when the sky cleared and the full moon shone, chilling winds of 18 knots made it unbearable to remain on the bridge.

The only thing that brought solace to me was when the Watch Leader, Bob, offered me the opportunity to steer LN. At that moment, the wind was blowing at 7 knots, and eight sails were unfurled in the moonlight. Those thirty minutes seemed to last forever, and I thoroughly enjoyed them.

Jorge on the helm.

At about 3 am I went downstairs to the kitchen to make a cup of milk tea, since I could barely feel my face or hands.

At 3.30 it was my turn to wake up the team in charge of the 4 am watch, so the only thing left to do was wait for them to arrive (you're supposed to arrive ten minutes before your watch begins) and then go to bed until breakfast at 0800.

From 10.30 to 11.30 was the so-called Happy Hour; then it was lunchtime – pesto spaghetti with salad – and back to write my 65-page logbook.

Thanks to the invitation that Fundación Escuela Goleta (www.escuelagoleta.org.ar) received from JST, some of its volunteers were able to participate in the legs that took place in the South Atlantic.

We had departed from Ushuaia, heading for Cape Horn, without having confirmed our permit to visit the Malvinas. For an Argentinian, arriving in the islands is "unfinished business". There were mixed emotions deep within my body: the first one was curiosity about visiting the Malvinas, getting to know its people and setting foot on a land I had never been to; the second one was pain, caused by knowing that young people of my generation had fallen when taking part in an unfair war.

That afternoon the wind blew like never before, with gusts above 30 knots, thus reaching the vicinities of Mount Pleasant at about 4 pm. It was then that the sails were lowered and our team took over the bridge, and it was my duty to steer into the channel. In that dreamlike state, I was touched by the significance of that beautiful experience, which I could not share with anyone who could possibly understand how I felt: an Argentinian was entering the Malvinas steering *Lord Nelson*.

It was curious, but so it happened.

Photo: Jorge San Martino

WELCOME TO
THE FALKLAND ISLANDS

HOT FRESH
FOOD HERE

Voyage 27 – Punta del Este to Punta del Este by Captain Barbara Campbell

Due to the change in joining port, the crew joined at different times. Training and briefings started at 0845 on 10th. We had hoped to sail at 1100, but sailing was delayed until after lunch, as it took the agents all morning to pay the Port Authority for the berth. Once clear of the port we set sails in light winds and sailed south. By 1700 we were becalmed and handed sail before anchoring close to Punta del Este.

The following morning we sailed off the anchor before smoko. For the remainder of the day we sailed westwards towards Piriapolis under Topsails and Fore Course. Just before lunch we wore ship and then anchored under sail for the night. No one can complain about a lack of manoeuvring the ship under sail as we weighed anchor, wore ship and anchored, without using engines all day. Rain was forecast but it set in early, just as the BBQ was lit! The evening was fast becoming a big sing-song in the bar, which luckily quietened down by 2200.

Next morning we had a happy half hour and a sail setting talk. The forecast had been for the SW winds to increase to 40 to 45 knots by evening. However, the wind quickly increased to 30 knots and we started dragging our anchor. We used the engines to hold our position and commenced weighing at 1050. The seas were building up and we had to brace the yards three times as we very slowly made our way out of the bay, making only a knot at times. We were far better out at sea than at anchor. Once clear, we set Topsails and Inner Jib and sailed 'full and by' in a southerly direction. By 1500 the wind was a steady 35 knots gusting to 50 knots. Due to the shallow waters of the Rio Plata, the seas quickly built up to a short steep swell. Big seas slapped against the ship's hull, sending water right over the ship. Safety lines were rigged and all external openings were shut as we resigned ourselves to an uncomfortable night. The locals all said this was a 'Pampero' blowing and blow it did. A force 8 to 10 blew all night. There was little sleep for anybody as the ship lurched and bounced with frequent heels to 45 degrees.

The Hand Sculpture at Punta del Este.

From 0400 13th, the wind started decreasing slowly. At 0830 we called 'All Hands' on deck, including the Engineers and the VC who were 'dead and dying' (aka seasick). We needed all of them to help wear ship in 40 knots of wind and big seas. With Cookie on the helm we wore ship and altered course to a NE'ly direction. Due to lack of sleep during the night I allowed the crew to sleep all day unless they were on watch. By 1700 the wind was down to 30 knots and decreasing. Most of the VC, even though seasick, managed to appear for watch, even though many were unable to eat.

From midnight we only had 15 knots of wind, which decreased to 10 knots by breakfast, when the crew were starving and in amazingly high spirits. They had not really expected the windy conditions. All the Argentinians and Uruguayans thought it brilliant that they had sailed in those conditions, as they had not previously realised just what it could be like. A real feeling of warmth and friendship flooded through the ship. At 1020 we commenced handing sail and started the engines as we were only twelve miles from Punta del Este. Berthing was a little tricky with a stern-first approach to the harbour and a little 'jig' around the end of the berth, but it went well. Even with the long breakwater, the swell came into the harbour and we had to rig wires in addition to mooring ropes. In the evening we had a last night meal which was a great success. Everyone got on so well and I was very proud to be the Captain of such a crew. The restaurant owner said he had never met so many people who had so enthusiastically enjoyed a holiday before.

From early morning on the 15th the crew started to leave. Those who lived locally and those who had a hotel booked for the night opted to stay back and help scrub the decks and clean the ship before we were open to the public.

The voyage was a resounding success. 92% under sail is a real achievement. The crew were wonderful, spirited and happy throughout and felt that the voyage had been very special.

Dates		Distances in Nautical Miles				Maximum Wind Force
Start	End	Total	Under Sail	Motor-Sailing	Motoring	
09.04.14	15.04.14	290	267	4	19	10

Beach and river plate Punta del Este.
Photo: David Mercer

Leg 8a

Punta del Este to Rio de Janeiro by Captain Chris Phillips

Leg 8a, Voyage 8b and Leg 8c replaced the originally-planned long passage from the Plate to Recife via Britain's most remote communities in Tristan da Cunha, St Helena and Ascension Island. Unfortunately low bookings made this promising voyage unviable, so an alternative programme of three voyages up the Brazilian coast was devised. Although it wouldn't have been my first choice to visit Rio again (ever!), with a decent berth arranged this time, and fuel bunkering arrangements improved, they turned out to

be successful voyages. Having been sailing from and travelling in South America for the best part of two months, perhaps I was also more attuned to the South American ways!

Leg 8a saw us departing from Punta del Este in Uruguay and sailing up past the border with Brazil, calling in at Sao Francisco do Sul, a very old port town which afforded us a welcome that was unbelievable. The local council organised a tour of the area for the voyage crew, and we received the mayor on board. I think they were slightly disappointed that we weren't staying for a week, but only a couple of nights!

Lord Nelson alongside at Punta del Este.
Photo: Marcin Dobrowolski

We sailed on from there to Ilhabela, which is a very pleasant island with a channel between it and the mainland, and is the centre of yachting in Brazil. We were well entertained ashore by the local yacht club, which offered its facilities, including pool and beach, to the crew.

From here we carried on to Ilha Grande, where we anchored in a very pretty bay for a barbecue. We had to leave that night straight afterwards due to one of the engines failing, so leaving us limping up the coast to Rio, where we berthed in the Marina da Gloria. This was far closer to the attractions than the Naval Base we used all those months past during our first disastrous visit.

Dates		Distances in Nautical Miles				Maximum Wind Force
Start	End	Total	Under Sail	Motor-Sailing	Motoring	
19.04.14	09.05.14	1218	496	220	502	7

Rio at sunset.
Photo: Marcin Dobrowolski

Voyable 8b – Rio de Janeiro to Rio de Janeiro by Captain Chris Phillips

This was a local voyage from Rio, during which we visited the port of Itajai, where we were welcomed alongside by a very loud band on the quayside, and the local council offered a free tour of the area. Thereafter we visited Ilhabela again, and again experienced uncertainty about whether we had to take a pilot. Clearance with the authorities there took an inordinately long time, given that we hadn't been outside Brazil, but eventually we were cleared and could let the crew ashore. We had a barbecue at the yacht club that evening. Our next stop was Ilha Grande once again, blissfully free of interference from the authorities, before heading back to Rio, taking a dismasted yacht in tow as we approached the port.

Flaking out the towing warp.

Photo: Marcin Dobrowolski

Dates		Distances in Nautical Miles				Maximum Wind Force
Start	End	Total	Under Sail	Motor-Sailing	Motoring	
10.05.14	23.05.14	886	240	273	373	7

Leg 8c

Rio de Janeiro to Recife by Captain Chris Phillips

Leg 8c was a very pleasant jaunt up the tropical part of the Brazilian coast, taking full advantage of the trade winds. We had several Brazilian voyage crew, which was very nice, including some young sea scouts. We managed to procure permission to visit the Abrolhos islands, which are a nature reserve, and voyage crew went ashore to visit both the lighthouse and the nature reserve. The next port was Maceio – not very exciting,

but still a nice place to stop for a break. We then went into Recife in time for World Cup Fever to kick in, and many of the crew joined in the street parties and festivities in this otherwise rather unprepossessing city.

Rio de Janeiro to Recife by Sheila Samuels

A few months ago, at one of our U3A Tuesday meetings, the guest speaker was Julia Ladds from the Jubilee Sailing Trust (JST). She told us that the JST had two tall ships (think of pirate ships), and that these were the only tall ships in the world specially designed for able-bodied and disabled people to join in every aspect of sailing, including being at the helm (even for the blind), or people just able to move one finger. She showed various photos, including a blind lady up on the rigging helping to fold away the sails. Please forgive me if my terminology is not correct.

I knew I had to do this, and at question time I asked if there was an age limit. Yes, it was a minimum of 16, with no upper age limit. At the end of the talk I spoke to Julia. She asked what problem I had, and I told her that seven and a half years ago I was hit by a car while crossing a road, which left me with fybromyalgia. I was surprised at how emotional I was. Now I had the possibility of an adventure, which I never thought could happen again.

Well, on the 9th May I flew to Rio de Janeiro to join The *Lord Nelson*. To say the cabin was compact was being generous. I shared with a young, delightful able-bodied 21-year old, who was my Buddy. Every disabled person had an able-bodied Buddy. Some brought their own Buddy. The disabled ranged from a beautiful 23-year old paraplegic, two in their thirties with MS, two permanently in wheelchairs with various debilitating illnesses; all with a sense of humour and a will to experience and enjoy life. Quite a few had sailed with JST before.

There were no passengers – we were all "Voyage Crew", and then there was the Permanent Crew. The next morning we were divided into our Watches. I was in the Forward Port Watch. Great, I now know the difference between Port and Starboard! We were instructed on ropes and sails and then, under guidance, put it all into practice. I found the best place for me was at the end of about six people, either pulling or releasing the ropes,

so that they just slipped through my hands, BUT I was part of the team.

Every day except Sunday we had Happy Hour from 11.00 – 12.00 am. This was when the ship was cleaned. The disabled were given jobs within their capability, and asked first if they could do it.

Each had a time sheet for the whole voyage, which showed when you were on watch on the bridge. This is when you had the opportunity to be at the helm, normally for 30 minutes at a time, and also take readings from the various clocks and dials. The radar could not always pick up small boats so you had to keep your eyes peeled for other ships and boats. Night watches would be from 8.00 pm to midnight, 12.00-4.00 am and 4.00-8.00 am. I liked the midnight – 4.00 am the best. The first few nights the night sky was cloudy, so when it was a starry night I was delighted. I could not believe what I was seeing. Port side stars were going around in a circle. I was mesmerised until someone laughed, and said it was not the stars that were moving, it was the ship.

When the ship is in full sail it is magnificent. Prior to going into port the Pilot Boat comes out and the pilot and another official come on board. Each time this happened they could not believe that a complete amateur was on the helm. Of course the Captain and Officers were on the bridge.

The first place we visited had a brass band to greet us, with South American and jazz music. More officials came on board, including one in a wheelchair, who had the biggest grin, not quite believing what he was seeing. For VC who cannot climb the rigging, it is possible to be hauled up in a wheelchair or Bosun's chair. I decided that I would ask to be sponsored, as I would not do this any other way. I was really frightened, and as I was being hauled up I kept saying "it is fan...tas...tic" and suddenly I realised it really was. I faced my fears and I can no longer say I am petrified of heights.

There are so many more experiences I could tell you about, but the most amazing one is that for the first time in seven and a half years I really do feel well, even though I still have the condition. I am standing taller. It is as though before this trip I had been living in a cage and now the cage has been smashed wide open!

Rio de Janeiro to Recife by Katherine Morris

2/6/14 – We anchored at the Abrolhos Archipelago, off the coast of Brazil, a Marine National Park and absolutely idyllic, and visited Ilha de Santa Barbara and Ilha Siriba. We had a tour from the lighthouse keeper, and saw many birds, including a red-billed tropicbird and lots of masked and brown boobies. That evening a few of us observed an interesting phenomenon of the setting moon; it was a horizontal crescent moon and as it slipped below the horizon, it left two devil horns sticking up!

Photo: Graham Woodhall

Photo: Lesley Sale

Dates		Distances in Nautical Miles				Maximum Wind Force
Start	End	Total	Under Sail	Motor-Sailing	Motoring	
27.05.14	12.06.14	1278	782	225	271	5

Photo: Katherine Morris

Leg 9

Recife to Halifax by Captain Barbara Campbell

Joining day was particularly busy; on top of briefings, we had to shift ship twice, take on food stores and, at 1400, a group of 32 young Sea Scouts unexpectedly arrived for a ship visit. Thankfully the PC were flexible. Training commenced straight after breakfast on 19th, finishing on the dot of 1400 so that the crew had time to make their way to the huge screen erected in one of the squares, to watch the World Cup match England v Uruguay which started at 1600. The jovial atmosphere alone was worth experiencing. Virtually all the crew

were hoping for England to win and no-one was more passionate than Marco, the Chief Engineer.

The Pilot joined at 0900 on the 20th and, once the last of the stores were on board and the Port Clearance papers in my hand, we were ready. Well, almost. The pilot insisted we make a tug fast both fore and aft to help with the turn. Now, this was the very same berth I had used in Leg 1 when I had neither pilot nor tugs, and I managed without either. As pilot and tugs were free, I went along with it and we came off the berth easily. The pilot and pilot boat crew particularly enjoyed the home-made birthday cake being handed out for morning smoko. We set sail as soon as possible and by lunchtime the engines were off. The 6.5 knots we were averaging was not as much as I had hoped.

The Main Royal and Main Course were added the following morning and the braces adjusted to try and go as fast as possible. During the afternoon and evening, the wind picked up from 20 to 30 knots SE'ly and our speed soared. Under a starlit night, with Mars, Saturn and Jupiter all visible at the same time, we sped along. We averaged 10 knots and touched 11.2 knots, much to the excitement of the VC. At speeds over 10 knots, an ethereal 'singing' starts in *Lord Nelson's* rigging. Overnight we kept up an average of 10 knots, with the ship truly in the grip of the 1.5 knot current, helping us on our way.

The crew enjoyed the great sailing and, with the sun shining, everyone had a smile on their face. We held a well-attended Sunday Service on the fore deck, with a quiet afternoon. This crew were fitness fanatics with keep-fit, stretching and yoga going on at various times of the day on different parts of the deck.

Early morning yoga at anchor.

Photo: Carol

Much of the 23rd June was spent in preparation for the 'crossing-the-line ceremony' due on the 24th. Unexpectedly we came out of the NW running current,

and, although we did not know this at the time, we were to remain in the south-bound eddy for the next seven days! In the evening the yards were braced three-quarters to port to take best advantage of the wind. Whilst bracing we caught a skipjack tuna, which came in handy for the next day's big event!

The crew were slightly on edge, not knowing exactly what was to happen as we crossed the equator at 0751. This was the first time *Lord Nelson* had been in the Northern Hemisphere in over 12 months. The 'crossing-the-line' ceremony was great fun, with the increasing number of crew who had crossed the line before dressed up as one of Neptune's court. I was Neptune and Jon, Mate, my Queen. Marco was the Barber, Cookie Derek the Surgeon, with Mike Snoxell as his assistant. Jim, 2nd Mate, did a great job as Pirate James Sparrow, who had captured *Lord Nelson* and locked up all her PC. About 34 'pollywogs', those who had not crossed the line at sea before, had their crimes read out. In turn they were each found guilty, had to kneel before Neptune in the paddling pool, kiss the tuna fish we had caught yesterday and have a spoonful of medicine (mashed bananas with a little curry powder and baked beans). They then had a small amount of hair cut off, though for the Permanent and Volunteer Crew, we were slightly harsher and shaved off an eyebrow. The bright blue-dyed oatmeal that was flung over the 'pollywogs' heads was not a resounding success

Captain Sparrow, Neptune, Neptunia and cohorts.

Photo: Professor Valerie Hazan

in that it stuck to everything, and, of course, Marco being Marco, upended the remaining contents of the medicine over the Queen and myself! After lunch, two hours were spent cleaning the ship following the morning's activities. The wind fell light mid-afternoon and we started engines. Four fillets from the tuna were then made into sushi by the Captain and one of the crew, a real treat.

The following day we clewed up the Courses and Royals and resigned ourselves to motor-sailing for the day. The PC held a Rescue from aloft drill, which served to keep the VC entertained. A solitary tropic bird flew around in the morning. The weather maps showed plenty of wind but it was all to the north of us – we just had to get there.

The wind flirted with us for a while on the 27th and we took advantage by re-setting the Courses and Royals and turned the engines off. At first we made 5 knots but by mid afternoon the wind had truly deserted us, so we started engines and handed all sail. Celestial navigation started that day and the watch average of four noon sights was only 1.7 miles out.

Low cloud with occasional torrential showers on the 28th were the order of the day. However it did not dampen the occasion of Eli's 21st Birthday. At breakfast time a pod of around 100 dolphins, the largest pod any of us had ever seen, surrounded the ship. We set sails and ran with the wind on the starboard quarter. Eli had a cake decorated by Vicki, the Medical Purser, and in the evening it was dry enough for everyone to have a wee toast to Eli on the Bridge. The Leadership @ Sea youngsters were in full swing with their 'disability awareness' and took it in turns to be in a wheelchair, be blindfolded or wear ear muffs. We sailed all day until the evening when the speed dropped to under 4 knots, forcing us to motor-sail overnight.

The game of 'Murder' started at 0900 on the 30th, and the crew quickly got into the swing of it. By 0930 when the Royals and Courses had been reset and the engines turned off, a number of crew had already been 'murdered'. The celestial navigation continued and the

watch were only a mile out. We were finally back in the favourable current and sailing nicely at 5 to 6 knots.

For the next three days we averaged 7 knots, and land was spotted a little after 0900 3rd July. Great excitement exuded from the VC, eager to get ashore. Under sail we passed through the mile wide channel to the north of Union Island, only clewing up at 1300 just before the turn to port into Chatham Bay, Union Island. We called up Vanessa from the 'Sun, Beach and Eat' bar and she became our taxi driver to Clifton to clear Customs and Immigration. The route was on one of the roughest tracks I have ever been on, consisting of rock and mud. The Immigration Officer was incredulous when I told him we had come from Brazil. He just could not understand why anyone would sail over 2000 miles and make Union Island their first stop; "there is nothing here" he protested. However we all thought that Chatham Bay with its rustic bars and beautiful beach, which we had all to ourselves, was 'paradise'. Back on the ship we had dinner at 1900, music on deck and an early night.

Alongside English Harbour, Antigua

Photo: Carol

Following breakfast we swam from the ship, a very pleasant experience with the seawater temperature at 28.5 degrees. We weighed anchor at 1100 and motored with fore and aft sail to Bequia. The berth was available from 1715, when the ferry departed.

Berthing was interesting with a stern-first approach to a 'blind' berth, and not much room to play with. Three ferries were moored stern-to on the end of the berth, screening the berth from view. The manoeuvre went well, and we moored with the stern only 30 metres from the beach.

All the crew were delighted we were alongside and we were barely tied up before the 'going-ashore' clothes came out. We celebrated our first alongside port with Caiparinhas. I showed the Harbour Master and the fire crew around, heavily laying on the disability card, and we managed to get a free berth. All but a handful of crew ate ashore, but most were tired and the village quiet, so there were no late nights.

Next day the crew were champing at the bit to get ashore after we had finished assisted climbs. Many took a tour of the island and ended up at one of the lovely beaches.

English Harbour from Shirley Heights.

Photo: Carol

Rain fell softly at dawn the following day, but cleared up in time for us to take the voyage photo. After more shore leave the crew were back for 1500 and Jim, 2nd Mate, took *Lord Nelson* off the berth. Once clear of Bequia, we had a very uncomfortable motor to the NE to pass to windward of St Vincent. At 2200 we were able to set sail and the motion settled down for a pleasant overnight sail.

We clewed up sail in the lee of St Lucia and motored past the iconic Pitons. At 1130 we set sails again to cross the channel between St Lucia and Martinique. Luckily we were only in the lee of Martinique for two hours before sailing to Dominica. At midnight we fell into the lee of Dominica, clewed up sail and motored slowly overnight.

At 0730, Topsails and Outer Jib were re-set for a gentle sail to 'Les Saintes', the attractive archipelago south of Guadeloupe. We sailed through the islets and were able to sail all but the last mile to an anchorage off "Pain du Sucre", a mini "Sugar Loaf". As we were only staying for a few hours we anchored close to the shore. Following an early lunch we ran the crew to the beach and most swam to the nearby reef, amongst plenty of colourful fish. It was a relaxing and lazy day for the VC. Everyone was back on board by 1540 and I gave instruction regarding sailing off the anchor; then we did just that. The engines were not even started. At 2000 we clewed up sail and slowly steamed northwards for a timed arrival off English Harbour, Antigua.

We passed Fort Berkeley, at the entrance to English Harbour, at 0830 on the 9th and proceeded inwards. The Harbour Master's assistant gave us poor information, first saying we were going stern-to. When I said we had agreed an alongside berth, he said we could go alongside but that we were to go head in, which I did not want. It was neither the time nor the place, in restricted waters, to get conflicting information. So we did not quite turn where I had planned, necessitating some quicker than usual engine orders to get alongside. The new 'Super Yacht berth' was a great berth for us. Clearing Immigration and Customs took two hours. A taxi driver came to see who wanted to go on a tour the following day and then the crew hit the beaches or watched the Argentina v Netherlands World Cup match.

On the 10th, 36 crew left at 0900 for a tour of the island, whilst the PC and BMs carried on with maintenance, including repairing the Outer Jib for the second time this voyage, and continuing painting the bulwarks.

Stores were ordered but while we were waiting for them we discovered that, due to an unpaid bill for *Tenacious* a year previously, the provisioning company would not release our stores. Fortunately this was resolved with help from Clare Cupples (ex-JST Captain living in the area). The stores finally arrived and we were singled up by 1130. Less than an hour later we were under sail, making 5 knots towards Anguilla. That afternoon we caught four fish, including a small tuna.

We rounded the north tip of Anguilla at 0830 on the 12th and braced the yards. At 1125 the port anchor was let go in Road Bay. The Immigration Officials were very cheery and let the VC come ashore straight away, before we were fully cleared in. The water was beautifully clear, the whole place understated and relaxed, a big hit with the VC. The crew had certainly gelled well and 'sundowners' were followed by dinner.

A blocked sea-water intake for the port generator delayed our sailing; there I was thinking it a ploy by the Chief Engineer who had wanted to delay sailing until the evening, in order to go ashore and watch the World Cup Final from a local hostelry! Yet again we sailed off the anchor, which everyone enjoyed, and out to the west, through Dog Island Passage before bracing the yards sharp and sailing 'full and by' to the north. Some of the crew were glad to be back at sea; others missed the beautiful Caribbean beaches. We set everything – all square sails together with fore and afters, including the Spanker.

A torrential rain shower and associated front passed over us at 0515 on the 14th, leaving us becalmed on a sea bereft of even a whisper of wind. The watch, the Mate and I handed all the canvas by 0600. Slowly the wind picked up and just before noon we were able to set sail again. However, this too was short-lived as, in the evening, our speed was down to 3 knots, so we clewed up square sails and motored for the remainder of the night.

At 0630 we reset sails, turning the engines off before breakfast and were soon cracking along in a great quarterly breeze. The watch were only 0.5 mile out

from the GPS at noon, or was it the other way round? In the morning we passed under the sun, so the sun was then bearing south at noon, instead of north.

On the 19th, the beautiful sandy beaches that fringe Bermuda came into view. The treacherous reefs around the island lay low and partly submerged. At 1500 we reached the Fairway Buoy, clewed up sail and motored through the stunning 'Town Cut' into St George's, a great protected harbour. By 1600 we were running mooring lines to Penno's Wharf. After completing Customs and Immigration formalities, we were free to go ashore. The local restaurant, 'Wahoo', became a firm favourite, as did the low key East End Mini Yacht Club. The crew had time ashore to enjoy the beaches. Some only got as far as nearby Tobacco Bay for some fabulous swimming and snorkelling, others managed the walk round the forts too. Three of our more mature crew rented bicycles and cycled all the way to Hamilton and back! St George's was definitely friendlier than Hamilton for a ship like *Lord Nelson*.

Fort Hamilton.

Photo: Carol

The 21st was busy as I had to finish repairing a sail, then the Acting Governor of Bermuda and Acting Mayor of St George's came to visit the ship. Fuel bunkers arrived late, following which I got a lift in a large tanker truck to go and pay the fuel bill at the depot! The gangway was being landed as I arrived back. However, we had a delay when the radar crashed yet again. With First

Mate Oli in charge, we let go our lines and turned off the berth. Just before we entered the buoyed channel, the Port Authority informed me we had not received our clearance papers. Usually they were brought to the ship but I had forgotten that we had not received them in the huge rush of the morning. So we took another turn and anchored in 'Powder Hole'. We all felt this was Bermuda's way of telling us to stay another day as we had had such a brilliant time. Mid-afternoon saw us motoring out through the beautiful 'Town Cut'.

We set sail just before breakfast the following morning and continued northwards. Our Cook, Derek, caught a beautiful Dorado fish. We set the remaining square sails plus the Spanker before lowering the DOTI boat into the water to take photos of the ship. After the photos were taken we held an impromptu Man Overboard Drill.

About 0200 on the 24th we entered the north wall of the Gulf Stream and by dawn were making 10 knots. Our speed increased to 13.7 knots, which delighted the crew. This was fast exhilarating sailing, helped by 30 knots of SW wind. By late afternoon the wind had dropped to 15 knots. For the first time all voyage, warm fleeces started appearing and there was porridge for breakfast, so it must have been getting cooler! Despite the speed dropping to 3 knots we managed to continue sailing. We clewed up sail after breakfast on the 25th as we were heading in a NE'ly direction. Motoring into headwinds was another reminder of the cooler climes.

On the 26th we sailed through the TSS off Halifax into the harbour. Under all square sail we passed through the narrow 0.2 mile wide gap between St George's Island and the busy waterfront by the Maritime Museum, looking splendid. All the crew were standing by as we had to hand sail promptly before anchoring for the night.

We weighed anchor after Happy Hour and made our way alongside the Tall Ships Quay, Halifax. Soon after our arrival, five members of the Canadian Border Security Agency arrived, together with our agent and Waterfront Development Corporation security guards.

The CBSA were pleasant but firm in all their dealings. The Canadian Authorities did not recognise the VC of *Lord Nelson* as crew and classified them as passengers. Unfortunately, one of our British Servicemen, sent by Help for Heroes, had a Ghanaian passport and was not allowed ashore.

At 0300 on the 28th, thick fog enveloped the port which proved to be an extensive bank covering much of south Nova Scotia and out to sea. As we hadn't called into Lunenburg as planned, we organised a coach to take the crew there for the day. Unfortunately the fog did not lift and, to make matters worse, it even rained. However the crew enjoyed Lunenburg, with its lovely historical wooden buildings and welcoming feel. They all visited the museum free of charge and had a lovely time. CBC news and radio, plus Global TV came down to interview various crew members. We had good prime time coverage. The crew enjoyed the sight-seeing as there was so much to see in Halifax, with all the museums and the historical dock area.

On the 31st we had groups from the CNIB and other disability groups looking around the ship, with a number of VC staying back to help.

Following my de-brief on 1st August, and a final happy hour, the time had come to say goodbye. It was an emotional departure for many, after 45 days on board. The voyage had been brilliant for just about everybody, in so many respects. There was great sailing (63% under sail); a great camaraderie amongst the crew; good weather; stunning Caribbean ports and all this mingled with plenty of sail setting and manoeuvring under sail. Many long-lasting friendships had been forged and I doubt there was a single crew member who did not take away more memories than they thought possible.

Summing it up, in the words of several VC: "This voyage far exceeded all expectations".

Watching England v Uruguay on the large screen in Recife.

Photo: Brian Rennie

Museum in English Harbour.

Photo: Carol

A sing-song in the bar.

Photo: Amy Derksen

Liberty boat, Caribbean style.

Photo: Carol

Dinner?

Photo: Carol

Lunenburg by horse and carriage.

Photo: Beth Hitchcock

Recife to Halifax by Katherine Morris – Cook's Assistant

24/6/14. 07:51 – We crossed the equator! The shellbacks (those that had previously crossed the line) had very secretively organised the ceremony for the pollywogs (those that had not crossed the line). We were a little apprehensive but it was all a lot of fun! Just very messy fun! We had our crimes read out to us in front of Neptune (Captain Barbara) and Neptune's wife (1st mate Jon). Being found guilty we had to kiss the fish…yes, an actual fish! We took our medicine and had a drink – both Cookie Derek's concoctions, definitely some curried banana in there somewhere! Then there was the shampoo – bright blue porridge, that's when it got really messy! We were cleaning up that blue porridge for days!

1/7/14 – I have enjoyed a lot of stargazing on my travels but nothing quite beats that first sighting of the North Star as we gradually headed north and day by day closer to home.

10/7/14 – In Antigua we were joined by the 'Tot Club', including ex-JST Captain Clare Cupples. We all stood out on the dock in a big circle and said a toast in naval tradition – "A bloody war and a sickly season; A bloody war and a quick promotion. And the Queen, God bless her!"

Recife to Halifax by Cate Prowse

When I went back to Brazil, I was itching for more sailing, after almost a year away. It was shocking how tired Nellie looked. Jobs we'd left undone in Freo were still unfinished, but the ship felt more than ever like a second home. Here were familiar jobs, things *I'd made* being useful on what was more than ever my ship.

Leg 9 was almost too good to be true. I would say it was the best crew I've ever sailed with, if it weren't for the many other awesome JST people I wish had been

there too. It was certainly the best sailing I've ever done. It was a charmed trip, across the equator, through the Caribbean to Halifax, Nova Scotia. I loved every minute of every day of that voyage and can remember everyone telling me I needed to stop, to sleep more, to take breaks. I didn't listen and spent many a watch dozing in the glaring sun, only to rush off the minute it was over to help the BMs with their next job.

Dates		Distances in Nautical Miles				Maximum Wind Force
Start	End	Total	Under Sail	Motor-Sailing	Motoring	
18.06.14	01.08.14	4218	2626	1437	155	7

Recife to Halifax by Jude Spenver-Gregson

Our Voyage on the Good Ship Nellie

Our journey on Nellie began some 38 days ago,
With expectations and excitement of a voyage we did not know.
After flights so long we arrived in Recife with relief,
never realising that locating Nellie would cause such grief.

Day two was spent on safety, sail briefing and taking on stores.
It was then off to the town square but, sadly, it was Ukraine that scores.

On day three we were up early, cast off, sails up and our sailing adventure had begun.
A crew member was huddled in a corner struggling to reason how 43 days at sea could be much fun.
The sea was choppy and a number of people were very unwell,
however they soon got used to the rock and the roll and the swell.

By day six we had got the watch system just about sussed,
and understood that good time keeping was an absolute must.
We quickly learnt that the many fixings on Nellie were not just complicated knitting and bundles of rope.
Buntlines, Clewlines, sheets, tack, halyards and sails with strange names; we'll soon make sailors, we hope.
Our daily cleaning on deck and below is known as happy hour:
clean heads, sweep floors and, best of all, use the hose to give feet a shower.

As days at sea went by we came to imagine what it would have been like in bygone times,
but, thanks to Derek's skills, our rations have not been ship's biscuits, weevils and limes.
We are all like baby gannets waiting for food in the nest,
the meals are so good it's hard to decide which dish is best.

Days in the southern ocean were sunny, steamy and very hot.
Some quickly gained a tan, and for others sun cream must never be forgot.

On the 26th June many assembled in the chart room to observe nought, nought, nought,
whilst others thought crossing the equator would be somewhat fraught.
The Shellbacks had spent days hatching a cunning plan;
it was shortly after breakfast that the fun began.
The stern platform was the court for King Neptune and his motley band,
The king pronounced the crimes so many and punishment was at hand.
The first of these penalties was to kiss the fish,
quickly followed by eating a spoon of some vile dish.
Our hair was cut and we drank some strange goo,
and not content, Pollywogs were all dyed blue.
Certificates were issued to new Shellbacks crossing the line,
this proof may be of use at some future time.

Our days were spent with sightings of flying fish, whales and the occasional dolphin pod,
and, of course fishing, but we won't be fined as catch was not cod.

After fourteen days at sea, sighting of land brought a cheer,
with Barbara promising an anchorage, a beach and a beer.
The Dotty boat put us on a beautiful sandy shore,
where most swam and some came to enjoy rum punches more and more.
We sailed past and visited many East Caribbean islands, south to the northern part.
Captain Barbara's voyage planning of sailing and island visits was quite an art.
After ten days relaxing in the Caribbean Isles,
Barbara announced we still had a journey of miles and miles.

The exact location of Bermuda was somewhat different to our old school book
and so we looked at the chart to check – seven days the journey took.
The apparent wealth and culture was so different from the Caribbean we saw,
however most set off to the most fantastic beaches to explore.

We have now been reminded of the northern climes: grey skies, rain and wind indeed.
Our attention was then focussed on a watch competition for speed.
Forward Starboard did its best at 12.6 knots overnight,
But, alas, we were beaten with 13.7 knots and we're sure it's right.

We give huge thanks and a cheer to Barbara and the permanent crew for giving us a voyage we will never forget,
For many all our starting hopes and dreams have been more than met.
For care, patience, great humour, teaching skills and making our trip such fun,
I am sure for many our allegiances with Nellie have only just begun.
Let us not forget our Watch Leaders who have kept us in order and good heart,
without whom I am sure we would have overslept and not played our part.
To our watch members, mess group and fellow crew:
thanks for the fun, laughter and friendships new.

May we share our wonderful experiences with family, friends and all we meet,
and tell all that sailing with The Jubilee Sailing Trust is such a great treat.

Celebration drinks at Halifax.
Photo: Professor Valerie Hazan

Voyage 28 – Halifax to Halifax by Captain Barbara Campbell

4th August – On this voyage we fell foul of Canadian Legislation. They deemed our VC as passengers and thus insisted we needed a Canadian Coastal Trading License. These take three months to obtain together with various surveys that are required. This meant that on this voyage we had to leave Canadian waters and call into a 'foreign port' before returning to Canada. The end result was that we said we would call into 'St Pierre and Miquelon', a little piece of France close to Newfoundland. St Pierre was 350 miles away, so to get there and back on a voyage of seven days (six nights) was a tall order. I was unhappy about this but we had to show we were taking the legislation seriously, so we sailed from Halifax straight after dinner on joining day, motoring eastwards overnight towards St Pierre. For the VC this felt rushed, particularly as moving around the ship at night was complicated by the fact that the watertight doors were closed due to poor visibility.

During the early morning of the 5th the fog descended, not unexpectedly, as this was the foggiest time of year. We finished our training at sea, carrying out 'Hands Aloft' and bracing practice as we motored eastwards, rolling gently in the light swell that heralded Tropical Storm Bertha. For several days we had been following her track as she was heading in our direction and due to pass about 120 miles off. It is not often that a Tropical Storm comes to the rescue, but Bertha did, 'big-style'. Due to the unpredictability of Tropical Storms and the fact that Bertha was associated with torrential rain which would massively impact on our radar picture, coupled with the thick fog (down to 50 metres) in the St Lawrence and St Pierre areas, we were able to legitimately change our plans and head for the port of Louisbourg in Cape Breton. To say I was delighted would be an under-statement. We turned round, setting sail late afternoon and sailed all the way to Louisbourg in light SW winds. The Port Authority in Louisbourg pulled out all the stops. When I first contacted them there was no room available, but they called me back to say they had moved the fishing boats around to enable us to use the end of the T-shaped berth.

Happy to be alongside.

Photo: Marcin Dobrowolski

We sailed until 1500 on the 6th when we clewed up sail and motored into the harbour. We wound our way in between the buoys, passed the impressive fort, and were secured alongside by 1730. The day was misty but the welcome warm. The press were waiting for us and interviewed several of the crew. In the evening a few of us ate at the 'Lobster Kettle' and then went to the nearby 200-seater 'Playhouse' where a brilliant band consisting of a fiddler, guitarist and pianist played Cape Breton and Celtic music. It was such a treat to listen to them, but even more of a treat when I invited them back to the ship and they played for a couple of hours in the bar.

Cape Breton band in our bar – a real treat.

Photo: Chris Tanlyn

The Captain with earplugs and safety goggles, ready to fire the cannon.

Photo: Julie Chinn

The morning of the 7th started with the Voyage Photo followed by assisted climbs. Of the four crew in wheelchairs, two were hoisted aloft whilst two used the self-ascend gear to haul themselves aloft. Local TV and radio filmed and recorded and we made the front page of the Cape Breton Chronicle. The few VC who had previously been to St Pierre said that we would have been treated as tourists there, whereas in Louisbourg we were welcomed into the community. Our berth fees were waived and volunteers from the fire brigade brought us water. The locals were delighted that we had visited and the crew thought it a great stop. Our friends Henry and Betty from Leg 1 came down and ran a shuttle service to the nearby fort. I arrived at the fort at 1530 to be asked if I had got the message that I was to fire the morning cannon. I clearly had not received the message, but they got special permission for me to fire the large cannon at the daily closing ceremony instead. I was given some training, dressed up in a thick felt greatcoat, with hat and woollen stockings, plus ear plugs, safety glasses and gloves. I marched down the 'streets' of the large fort with the cannoneers, to the beat of the drums. I was the 'little one', with baggy stockings round my ankles, trying, but failing, to match the long strides of the cannoneers! The VC thought it was a hoot – after they had recognised me! Three-quarters of a pound of black powder was loaded through the muzzle of the cannon. At the word 'fire' I lifted the linstock, a wooden staff holding a length of smouldering 'slow match', and lowered the smouldering rope to the 'touch hole' on the cannon. The deafening explosion which followed triggered a multitude of camera clicks. Throughout our visit, the locals thought it wonderful that we had chosen their port to visit.

Two drummers from the fort came down to the quay and played the drums as we departed the following morning. Once clear of the berth, we braced the yards and set fore and aft sail. Off the fort we stopped engines, setting the square sails. In return the fort fired the cannon for us! We continued sailing slowly out of the port. The wind picked up against us and we had to start engines and motor towards Halifax.

In the early morning of the 9th, the wind filled in to a gentle breeze from the NE. We set Topsails and fore and aft sail and were able to sail for a couple of hours.

The Captain's dinner!

Photo: Jon Garvin

But it was not to last; we handed sail before lunch then motored to Halifax in bright sunshine. Oli, the Mate, brought the ship nicely alongside, and we had a late dinner after the gangway was rigged.

Following the Captain's debrief on the 10th, there was sign off, a final happy hour and smoko before the VC departed.

Despite the lack of sailing it had been a great voyage and one VC who had sailed many times said it was her favourite. The trip was made by the call into Louisbourg where we were taken into the hearts of the locals. The VC all gelled, and. together with the PC, this created a fun atmosphere.

Spot our Captain?
Photo: Julie Chinn

186

Photo: Chris Tamlin

Halifax to Halifax by Katherine Morris – Purser

6/8/14 – The evening's entertainment was provided by "Kintyre Lite" (Jennifer Roland, Jason Kemp and Mark MacIntyre) at the Louisbourg Playhouse. Off stage the crew of Nellie also provided much entertainment with lots of dancing and silliness! After making friends with the band, we invited them back for some more merriment; a delightful musical night continued in the bar!

7/8/14 – On our visit to the Fortress of Louisbourg, Captain Barbara joined the Cannoneers, donned their uniform and was given the honour of lighting the fuse of the 18th Century cannon. The team at Louisbourg also arranged for two 18th century French soldiers to attend our departure, playing their piccolo and drum as we departed. And, as we sailed away, we were saluted by traditional cannon fire.

Photo: Julie Chinn

Dates		Distances in Nautical Miles				Maximum Wind Force
Start	End	Total	Under Sail	Motor-Sailing	Motoring	
04.08.14	10.08.14	416	75	50	291	n/k

Leg 10

Halifax to London by Captain Chris Phillips

The published itinerary for this voyage, returning home via Iceland and the Faroe Islands, was a very exciting one, and I'm sure it was the reason many voyage crew signed up (as well as the anticipation of our triumphant return to the UK up the Thames into the heart of our capital). Unfortunately it became evident during the early days of the voyage that the distances involved, and the speed required in order to make any meaningful length of stops in either country, made the plan nigh on impossible to execute. Also, a feature high

on my watch list while planning the voyage was the ominous presence of hurricane Cristobal. This, as we left Halifax, was already brewing many hundreds of miles to the south in the Caribbean.

Still, at the time of departure from Halifax, I was as keen as anyone to make the plan work, so after a brief overnight stop and bunkering in Lunenburg (once the Canadian customs had reassured me that we were allowed to remain in Canada for an extra night after departing Halifax), we sailed east towards the Atlantic, passing south of Sable Island (made famous by the film *The Perfect Storm*). However, once I had gained a realistic appraisal of the weather conditions and our likely progress, I decided that we simply could not follow the northern route without an unacceptable risk of missing our arrival deadline in London for the planned welcome festivities. I thus planned an alternative route via the Azores, which would still give us an interesting (and much warmer) port stop mid-voyage, and slightly more flexibility for timing. My voyage report only mentions Cristobal once, but he was very much in my mind as I made this decision; rightly as it turns out, as unusually for a tropical revolving storm, instead of burning himself out and recurving harmlessly (for us) out into the Atlantic somewhere off the Carolinas, he continued up the eastern seaboard and followed the exact route we would have taken towards Iceland. Never have I felt more justified in changing the plan.

Alongside Horta, Faial.

Photo: Marcin Dobrowolski

It was a mixed voyage from the point of view of sailing – we had a fair amount of good sailing from Nova Scotia to Horta, but after the Azores we had to motor into NE'ly winds for the entire way, and by way of a StW finale, battle our way up the English Channel against a NE'ly gale. It was only by virtue of a timely lull in the wind that we were able to push on up to the Dover Straits and get into the Thames Estuary in time for the grand procession up to Tower Bridge, with

just a short overnight breather anchored off Southend Pier. We met *Tenacious* as we passed her overnight berth at Tilbury Landing Stage, picked up our pilot at Gravesend and headed upriver.

It was worth the battle: as we passed under Tower Bridge's famous span, our arrival home was heralded by four Royal Marine bandsmen sounding a bugle fanfare from the bridge's caissons. Unbeknown to me, the bridge was actually lifted by Andy Spark, our Ship Operations Manager. We swung just upstream of *HMS Belfast*, and glided gently alongside to the strains of the Band of HM Royal Marines, and a welcoming committee of friends, family, JST trustees and staff and representatives of our sponsors. Once the gangway was rigged – quite a performance as it turned out – JST President the Hon Jacquetta Cator was first across the brow to welcome home her daughter Lizzie Thistlethwaite, who had been a crew member on the voyage.

The day, the voyage and, for me at least, Sail the World, was rounded off by the official Norton Rose Fulbright-sponsored homecoming reception in their London headquarters just around the corner: a fitting finale to such a ground-breaking odyssey.

Previous visitors to Horta.

Photo: Marcin Dobrowolski

Photo: Peter Cairns

Royal Marine trumpeters
on Tower Bridge.

Halifax to London by Cate Prowse

Shortly before Leg 10 left for England, we became aware that there was a shortage of medical pursers. I am not sure what criteria were used to select JC and me to fill in as "non-medical pursers" (perhaps longest and second-longest amount of time spent on StW trips) but we embraced the role eagerly. We had matching T-shirts, were ruthless about Happy Hour, and learnt the washing machine's cycle more or less by heart. I still meet people who were on that voyage and they invariably complain we were the harshest enforcers of Happy Hour, as we scrambled to get the ship looking her best for her return. Like my previous Atlantic crossing captained by Chris Phillips, Leg 10 was plagued by bad weather (first an unnaturally northern hurricane, then no wind or bad wind all the rest of the way). Still it was easy to stay good humoured, even when my job included glamorous tasks like toilet brush bleaching.

The PC were, as ever, fantastic and, to top off the day, arriving in London with *Tenacious* behind us, in time for a wild party courtesy of our sponsors, seemed a perfect end to my time on Sail The World. When I joined I was a novice, with only one other tall ship trip under my belt. I left with so many experiences, having done many jobs, including ones not officially open to voyage crew. I also have a bucket list of places I want to go, from all the other stories I've heard, about voyages I missed.

Alongside Horta, Faial.

Photo: Dr Tom Everett

Halifax to London by Peter Cairns – Watch Leader

I was introduced to the JST by Beryl Whipp (aka Lord Nelson), who was the nursing sister at J H Fenner in Hull, where I worked at the time. My only prior experience of tall ship sailing was in early 1989 on *STS Malcolm Miller*. My first voyage with the JST was in June 1989, from Leith to London.

To date I have sailed on 57 voyages, 522 days, covering over 38,800 nautical miles, sailing on both *STS Lord Nelson* and *SV Tenacious*. I got my RYA Yachtmaster qualification in 1991, and first sailed as a Watch Leader in 1992. I have visited many ports on voyages in England, Scotland, Ireland, Wales, Channel Islands, Lundy, Scilly Isles, Isle of Man, Inner & Outer Hebrides, Orkney, France, Belgium, Netherlands, Denmark, Portugal, Spain, Canary Islands, Madeira, Azores and Canada.

As well as sailing, I was the East Yorkshire JST branch secretary for about 12 years. During this time I helped organise several port visits to Hull, including getting free provisions for the ship. Over the years I have spent many weeks as a maintenance volunteer on both ships. I also did two Shorewatch weeks, helping in the construction of *Tenacious*, and was a Watch Leader on the shakedown voyage in August 2000.

I am albino and registered blind, with about 5% vision in my good eye. The JST has given me the confidence to run a watch and encourage watch members to push themselves beyond their comfort zone, often in a challenging and hostile environment. I have witnessed many life changing experiences of voyage crew over the years, in both the young, old, disabled and able-bodied.

As the duty watch on *Lord Nelson's* return to London at the end of Leg 10, I had the honour of helming *Lord Nelson* through Tower Bridge and alongside *HMS Belfast*.

Peter helming through Tower Bridge.

Halifax to London by Jess House

I first heard about the JST when a brochure all about the Sail the World voyages dropped onto our doormat for my mum (she is a doctor and Watch Leader for the JST). I found that the only voyage I was able to do (due to age and school time) was Leg 10, so I asked mum if I could do it, and she said that if I raised the funds myself, then yes, I could go. So I did and off I went! I applied when I was 14 and at the time it felt like a very long way off, but the time flew by and here we all are three years on.

I have lots of gossip from our voyage: I got my GCSE results on board (which were 4A*s, 5As and 1B) over satellite phone, just off Sable Island about 100nm off the coast of Nova Scotia. BMs Alan, Neil and Godfrey rescued a fender and a lot of rope, serving as a habitat for goose barnacles and queen scallops as well as sargasso weed, which later made up the ship's aquarium in a glass jar! The Great Egg Drop with all the 'eggscruciating' puns thrown in is always a good one to mention, with the kilts and other items of clothing

(absent and present). As part of Leadership @ Sea, Aoife and I made a logline and presented it to the crew, as well as watch-leading, controlling sail setting and paying special attention to parts of the ship which have been specially adapted to allow for 100% accessibility.

Jess and her fish.

I also made a heaving line (which is still there and was used recently!) and learnt how to splice and do whippings. I caught a Dorado which meant that the scores were Jess 1: Chipps 0 (Chipps was the Second Engineer).

In the Azores the restaurant called the Hot Rocks was really interesting where they brought out real stones (as opposed to electrically heated ones) heated to an amazingly high temperature on which to cook the raw meat yourself – I really loved that.

There was a crisis on board when all the proper tea bags ran out and we were left with the very bland Brazilian ones which were bought in bulk when the ship was there. Cheese and biscuits were eaten at 0400 before the early watch started, and jam roly poly was also consumed before the midnight – 0400 by various members of my watch (and me!). Neil would often make us popcorn for our night watches which was always well received – often by the sea as well as us ravenous watch-keepers! I have in my diary that on one of the days, Godfrey had no less than 10 pieces of chocolate cake; I think that's worth mentioning!

There were three birthdays I can remember: Markus Strydom, James Whale and Mary Utting all had theirs on board, and delicious cakes were enjoyed by all. Not many of the VC were actually seasick, but the only time I felt slightly queasy at sea was from licking the toffee pots whilst helping Cookie Dave make banoffee pie. Does that count?

We had a feathery friend who hitched a lift for about three days before sadly

BMs Godfrey Jones, Alan Fisher and Neil Marshall.

passing on, and a burial at sea took place. Dolphins were spotted in the Channel and swam with the ship for about three quarters of an hour, which was spectacular!

There were two inter-watch quizzes and then of course the SODS (Ship's Operatic and Drama Society) Opera on the last night, which was full of hilarity.

Peter Cairns (one of the Watch Leaders) was the helmsman taking Nellie through Tower Bridge, which was particularly amazing because he is registered blind. The Spanker was stowed on our way up the Thames before going under Tower Bridge to moor alongside *HMS Belfast*. Then on the last night after the party Steve told me I was going to be a Bosun's Mate, which was and is one of the best things that has ever happened to me.

Dates		Distances in Nautical Miles				Maximum Wind Force
Start	End	Total	Under Sail	Motor-Sailing	Motoring	
14.08.14	20.09.14	3679	677	2440	562	7

Great egg race winners.

Are we nearly there yet?

Note from Alan Fisher

One of our crew members was Marcus Strydom, a larger than life man originating from South Africa. During the voyage, we discovered that he had always wanted to follow in his father's footsteps and join the military, which he did. He joined the British army, and finished as a Lance-Sergeant in the 1st Battalion Grenadier Guards. In further conversation we found out that on his second tour in Afghanistan he was shot twice and blown up by a hand grenade. His thoughts at the time were "this day can't get any worse".

For his acts of bravery he was awarded the Military Cross by the Queen on the 21st May 2013. His full citation can be read on: www.britishempire.co.uk/forces/armyunits/britishinfantry/grenadiermarcusstrydom.htm.

A very brave man.

Marcus Strydon

Approaching Tower Bridge
Photo: Alan Fisher

Voyage 10a – London to Southampton by Captain Barbara Campbell

The 'Norton Rose Fulbright Sail the World Challenge' ended in London with *Lord Nelson* moored alongside *HMS Belfast*, a stone's throw from NRF offices, where a great party was held for us. But for most of the *Lord Nelson* crew, the final leg to Southampton was to close the circle and complete the circumnavigation back to our home port.

The VC joined *Lord Nelson* in the stunning setting of the Pool of London on the 22nd September. Most of them had sailed on Leg 10 or one of the previous StW legs, but we had to remain aware that a few VC who had not sailed before still needed all the training. It was a busy old day, with joining between 1000 and 1030. The pilot boarded at 1200. Timings were spot on and we proceeded through Tower Bridge at1330. As always, it was a magnificent sight to see one of our ships framed by Tower Bridge. Shortly after 1600 we briefly went alongside Tilbury Landing Stage to fill the fresh water tanks and to allow the pilot to disembark. We motored

further downstream, anchoring for the night in Leigh Small Ships anchorage, close to Southend Pier.

We weighed anchor before breakfast the following morning to get a little further east before the flood tide kicked in. Sails were set at 1330; when we were north-

Alongside *HMS Belfast*.

198

Motoring up Southampton Water.
Photo: Max Mudie

though it was early afternoon, all the crew realised that we had made the very best use of the winds. During the afternoon we took the Voyage Photo, followed by assisted climbs. Tired but happy, we enjoyed a quiet night at anchor.

On Friday 26th September, the wind was forecast fair for sailing up to berth 106, Southampton. However, once underway, the wind had other plans and we had to content ourselves with motoring with fore and aft sails set. Friends, family and office staff mingled on the quay, creating a lovely atmosphere as we came alongside our berth. For many of the crew, our arrival at Southampton marked *Lord Nelson* truly coming home, having gone 'full circle' and more, around the world.

east of Margate, we sailed to windward of the Thanet Wind Farm before calling all hands to wear ship off 'The Falls'. Once round on the other tack we ended up heading back towards the wind farm! At 1730, we handed sails, and altered to a S'ly course, towards the Traffic Separation Scheme. The lights of Dover were abeam at 2130 and we continued in the south-west bound lane for the remainder of the night.

After a quiet night at sea we were south of Shoreham at breakfast. After smoko, once the floodtide and head winds had eased off, we set sails. For the remainder of the day we sailed in a SSW direction across the Channel, under Topsails, Courses and Fore T'Gallant. The morning showers disappeared and the sun tried to break through in the afternoon. We handed sail at 2200 in order to motor back across the Channel.

With Swanage in sight, sails were set before breakfast the following morning, then, with wind and tide in our favour, we sailed to the Needles Channel. We had a brilliant sail past the Needles, up through the Solent, and, to my delight, all the way to the anchorage, near the mouth of the Hamble river. We handed the last of the sails as the anchor was let go, and

Andy Spark, Ship Operations Manager, taking our first mooring line, back home in Southampton.
Photo: Max Mudie

	Dates		Distances in Nautical Miles				Maximum Wind Force
	Start	End	Total	Under Sail	Motor-Sailing	Motoring	
	22.09.14	26.09.14	326	81	35	210	5

Sue Tupper welcoming "Nellie" back.

Sailing the World!

Hello, my name is James Whale. I want to tell you about my experiences with the Jubilee Sailing Trust (JST). JST is a charity funded to take disabled and able bodied people aged 16 right up to 80 or even 90 years old, out to sea for sailing experiences. This is a short article on my personal experiences on the two ships, the *Lord Nelson* and *Tenacious*.

My first trip was a 5 day trip for my 21st birthday which I was really excited about. I always remember my first trip; it was from Poole to Southampton for five days on *Tenacious*. We could not sail until the second day because of bad weather. At first I was itching to get out sailing but then when we were actually going out to sea, I realized there was a very good and valid reason why the captain stayed in port. Then I felt the nerves!

In October 2012 I set off with 39 other crew members on the *Lord Nelson* for a trip around the world. JST's ships are the only tall ships in the world to show other countries what you 'can do' rather than what you 'can't do' even with a disability.

The first leg was to Rio – we stopped in Las Palmas and then sailed on down the Atlantic, across the equator and to Brazil.

Crossing the equator is fun because you get gunged. People who have not crossed the line before are known as 'Pollywogs' and you are "punished" for small crimes. I had spilt some water over the charts. You are found guilty by Lord Neptune and ordered to take the plunge! You are then designated a 'Shellback' and you can enjoy watching other Pollywogs waiting their turn.

I spent Christmas in Rio on a very hot beach before I left the ship and flew home. The ship then sailed to Cape Town – Durban-Kochi and to Singapore, where I rejoined it. I then sailed across the equator again, sailing to Bali, the Cocos Islands and eventually Fremantle in Australia.

James climbing the mast – everyone works on board – this is no cruise!

Although this trip was not as long as the Rio trip, this time we had force 10 gales and at times I thought we could have capsized. It was so rough we could not go to Christmas Island as planned and I was so glad to get to Fremantle near Perth (Australia). I had to laugh when I was watching Australian TV and it was their winter. They were reporting about the cold snap across Australia, saying the temperatures were plummeting below 20 degrees! And how to stay warm. I was in shorts and T-shirt!

A special thank you to everyone at St Peter's, Maer who prayed for my safe voyages – It's great to know people are thinking of me.

James with friends and the Paralympic torch which the ship was presented with prior to leaving Southampton.

destination was Horta; a cold Arctic destination in the Azores where temperatures average 17 degrees!

Horta was the last stop before the big homecoming in London, where we had a great reception through Tower Bridge and there were lots of media people. We came alongside *HMS Belfast* to celebrate a marvellous adventure, and to join in the party hosted by our sponsors, Norton Rose Fulbright.

Overall the JST experiences have been fantastic for me, especially the Sail the World voyages. I have been to wonderful places and met some amazing people, including many injured servicemen as Help for Heroes has been nominating people for these voyages, giving these people a chance to experience adventure.

The ship then went on around Australia to Sydney, where it took part in the tall ship race to Auckland. Then it crossed the southern Ocean, taking a trip down to Antarctica before sailing up through Argentina, Uruguay and Brazil.

I re-joined the ship and sailed up the coast past the mouth of the Amazon, Venezuela through the Caribbean, Eastern USA to Canada where I had two weeks in Halifax with my Aunt Carolyn and Uncle Steve. Whilst being away from the ship, we went shopping for hats, scarves and thick jumpers and Icelandic Kroner currency – all set for the frozen north.

When I got back on board everybody else was also ready for Iceland. But the captain told us that a volcano had erupted in Iceland, and a hurricane was tracking that way; it would be too dangerous to sail there. We had even tried on the immersion suits which they only do for Arctic trips. But the big freezing Arctic

Alongside *HMS Belfast*.
Photo: Peter Cairns

Welcome Home Party Speech 26 September 2014

by Captain Barbara Campbell

We have now come 'full-circle', back to our home port of Southampton. On the 21 October 2012, Trafalgar Day, we sailed away and out through the Needles Channel. Nearly two years later, once again under canvas, we came up the Needles Channel. In the intervening time, *Lord Nelson* has covered 52,557 nautical miles, equivalent to 60,482 land miles.

Unlike the ships of yesteryear, we do not have a large professional crew, as our crews are largely untrained, but abounding in enthusiasm. Together we have sailed the ship, and when you are battling against the winds, you appreciate just how vast the oceans really are. When I flew home on leave and covered the miles so easily, I reflected on how much effort it had taken us under canvas. Sometimes, with seas running down the decks, we really fought for each mile. *Lord Nelson* proved herself a true work-horse of the seas. Unlike our forefathers, we were not racing across the oceans delivering valuable cargoes of silk and spices, but we sailed the very same waters and sprinkled a little JST magic along the way.

For the JST, sending a ship around the world entailed many pioneering moments. On the way to Rio we crossed the equator for the first time. We must have enjoyed it so much, as we crossed it another five times. I am not sure whether the PC or the VC had most fun in the Crossing the Line ceremonies. Why is it that all the PC want to dress up with big boobs?

There were two teams of Permanent Crews, one on the ship and one on leave. We have all come back older and wiser, after having been sorely challenged at times.

Nearly every voyage featured a call into a remote island, like Fernando de Noronha and The Abrolhos Islands off Brazil, Cocos Island off Australia, Union Island in the Caribbean, a mini paradise, and the Falkland Islands. But it was probably Antarctica which topped the bill. Many of these islands are rarely visited and our crews found them delightful.

Along the way, we had fun times, like when we had torrential tropical rains and some of the crew even washed their hair in the scuppers. We also made the video epic 'I want to break Fremantle', where, yet again, the PC got to dress up!

We were privileged to see colourful sunsets and turquoise seas. In the skies, blue and red footed boobies and albatrosses were our companions, while whales and dolphins graced us with their presence.

But we did not get round without encountering our fair share of storms. The biggest of these, with over 60 knots of wind, were approaching Fremantle, crossing the Drake Passage and the Bass Strait. Approaching Fremantle, our speed reached 14.2 knots under sail, the fastest, we think, that LN has ever gone. In the storms, it is the galley staff who suffer most. Keeping food in containers, on the cooker, on plates, in bowls is an art. As is the amazing mess when a whole tray of banoffee pie flies off in a gale, or two litres of cream splatters all over the upper mess.

In Kochi, India, we met up with our sister ships *Tarangini* and *Sudarshini*. They may have been better painted than *Lord Nelson*, but we set our sails better and it was evident they do not go to sea as often as we do.

We witnessed wonderful warm welcomes in Cape Town, Australia, New Zealand, Canada and the Falklands. However, Argentina and Brazil, with their exorbitant costs and red tape were a slightly different story.

We met up with three Dutch tall ships in Fremantle and sailed together to Adelaide, Melbourne, Hobart, the Fleet Review in Sydney and the race to New Zealand. Crossing the Bass Strait from Hobart, we were caught in the same storm. They suffered broken spars and masts whilst our 21 year-old main Course sail met its demise.

Our PC and VC have achieved so much; they have risen to the occasion time and again. Our VC wrote fabulous blogs to keep friends and family interested back home. We have sailed the World,…. but we're all glad to be home.

Conclusion by Alan Fisher

What started out as a dream in November 2011 ended with a jubilant return to Southampton in September 2014, with *Lord Nelson* having completed a circumnavigation, crossed the equator six times and sailed 52,557 nautical miles. Plans evolved, changes were made, many exciting countries were visited and world-wide friendships made. Over a thousand adventurous people took part in the thirty voyages, and have life-long memories to cherish.

The Jubilee Sailing Trust continues to thrive: Sail the World uncovered numerous new, exciting opportunities. The Trust has officially established a presence in Australia, with a new operation based in Melbourne, and supporters from the region have already made a very significant fundraising contribution.

Given this resounding success, it was the obvious place to start the JST's international expansion. To mark this fantastic development, and to celebrate her 15th anniversary, *Tenacious* embarked on an international tour, visiting some of the world's most exciting sailing destinations, including the Caribbean, Panama Canal and South Pacific Islands, arriving in Melbourne in August 2016.

This development will provide even more opportunities for able-bodied and disabled people to enjoy life-changing tall ship sailing adventures on board the *Lord Nelson* and *Tenacious*.

Lord Nelson leading *Tenacious* into London.
Photo: Mike Travis

Abbreviations Used

AC	Air Conditioning
BM	Bosun's Mate
CA	Cook's Assistant
DAFF	Department of Agriculture, Fisheries and Forestry
DoTI/DOTI	Department of Trade and Industry (Ship's Boat)
Heads	Toilets
HRA	High Risk Area
IACH	International Association of Cape Horners
IED	Improvised Explosive Device
JST	Jubilee Sailing Trust
Kn	Knot
LN	Lord Nelson
M	Sea (Nautical) Mile
MCA	Maritime and Coastguard Association
MP	Medical Purser
PC	Permanent Crew
RIB	Rigid Inflatable Boat
Smoko	Tea Break
STS	Sail Training Ship
SV	Sailing Vessel
U3A	University of the Third Age
VC	Volunteer Crew/Voyage Crew
W/L	Watch Leader